WRITERS AND THEIR WORK

ISOBEL ARMSTRONG
General Editor

HENRY IV

WW

William Shakespeare

HENRY IV

Laurence Lerner

© Copyright 2008 by Laurence Lerner

First published in 2008 by Northcote House Publishers Ltd, Horndon House, Horndon, Devon PL19 9NQ, United Kingdom.
Tel: +44 (01822) 810066 Fax: +44 (01822) 810034.

British Library Cataloguing-in-Publication Data
A catalogue record for this book is available from the British Library

ISBN 978-0-7463-1191-2 hardcover
ISBN 978-0-7463-0851-6 paperback

Typeset by PDQ Typesetting, Newcastle-under-Lyme
Printed and bound in the United Kingdom

Contents

Preface

This book is divided into three unequal parts – unequal in length and (arguably) unequal in importance. Part 1 is a piece of straightforward history, with some historiographical reflections: it narrates the events of Henry IV's reign, tries to describe the political situation in England in the first fifteen years of the fifteenth century, and describes briefly how these events were seen by the chroniclers who related them. Part 2, which is the longest, offers a reading of Shakespeare's two plays. Part 3 discusses their reception, from their first appearance in the 1590s to the present. It concentrates especially on our own time, as is the policy in *Writers and their Work*; it does not, however, limit 'our own time' to scholars and critics now writing, but deals with Shakespeare criticism since it became a serious academic concern in the mid-twentieth century, and thus offers a brief survey of how changing intellectual fashions have influenced the interpretation of a Shakespeare play.

1

Before Shakespeare

'Uneasy lies the head that wears a crown'; and crowned heads were not the only ones to be uneasy. If we are feeling depressed about the extent of violence in the modern world, it can be salutary to learn something about the state of England in the fifteenth century, a time of almost constant violence.

In 1399 King Richard II was deposed by his cousin Henry Bolingbroke. Henry had been exiled by Richard in the previous year, at first for ten years, then the sentence was changed to life. In changing the sentence, Richard also seized his estates, whereupon Henry landed in England with an army. He was supported by several nobles, including Henry Percy, Earl of Northumberland. Richard was in Ireland at the time, engaged in the endless task of suppressing rebellion in that hardly governable country; and when he returned his army deserted him, so that he was unable to put up any resistance, and was captured at Flint castle. Brought back to London, he was compelled to resign the crown, and Bolingbroke became Henry IV. Richard was imprisoned in Pomfret Castle, from which he never emerged alive.

Richard's reign had had its problems and disturbances; Henry's was worse. Constantly short of money, he also had an insecure claim to the throne that he had usurped. He was of course a member of the royal family, descended from King Edward III, but his father, John of Gaunt, was Edward's fourth son, and Lionel of Clarence, the third son, had had a daughter, Philippa, whose son, Roger Mortimer, Earl of March, had actually been proclaimed as Richard's heir. Roger was dead, but his young son Edmund, then aged 9, could be considered the rightful king.

There was constant trouble in the Celtic fringe. In the north, Archibald Earl of Douglas with his Scottish followers was in intermittent conflict with the Percy family: they defeated him at Humbledon (or Holmedon) in 1402, but this led to a quarrel with King Henry about the ransoming of prisoners, and when this quarrel later flared into open rebellion, Douglas joined with the Percys.

Much more serious trouble came in Wales. Wales, which had been conquered by Edward I in the thirteenth century and incorporated into England, was treated as a colony: the English and the Welsh had different legal systems and different inheritance practices, there was little intermarriage, and Richard had rewarded his friends by giving them Welsh estates. The situation was described as 'the madness of the Saxon barbarians who have usurped the land of Wales' by a Welsh squire called Owain Glyn Dwr, who proclaimed himself Prince of Wales in 1400. Before long, he was the leader of a war of independence

For several years the Welsh rebels were very successful. They had the advantage always enjoyed by guerilla fighters who know their own terrain much better than their rulers do. Their most famous success was in a pitched battle at Bryn Glas, near Pilleth, which became famous because of the rumours, widely circulated and believed by the English, that after the battle the dead English soldiers had been luridly mutilated by Welsh women; and Edmund Mortimer, younger brother of Roger (and uncle to the boy Edmund who had a strong claim to the throne), who was in command of the English forces, was not only captured by Owain, he then defected to the Welsh cause, and married Owain's daughter.

King Henry made three expeditions into Wales, all without success. He appointed two of the Percy family as regents in Wales: Thomas, Earl of Worcester, Northumberland's brother, in the south, and Northumberland's son, also called Henry, and known as Hotspur because of his military prowess, in the north. But the Percys, always difficult to handle, finally turned against the king and broke into open rebellion. They were defeated, and both Worcester and Hotspur were killed at the battle of Shrewsbury in July 1403. But this did little to halt the Welsh cause: the seriousness of the rebellion can be judged from the fact that for three years or so virtually no revenues were collected by the English government in Wales. A large army sent by Henry against the Welsh had to be recalled because of news of a rebellion in the north of England, led by Archbishop Scrope; the Archbishop was tricked into surrendering, and executed in 1405. The Earl of Northumberland was finally defeated, and killed, at the battle of Bramham Moor in 1408.

It is very difficult to estimate the success of Owain's rebellion, since it usually avoided pitched battles, and its main weapon was the refusal to cooperate with the English authorities. Its high point was probably in 1405-6, when he had been able to enlist the help of France (a French force actually landed at Milford Haven in 1405), and signed a treaty, known as the Tripartite Agreement, with Edmund Mortimer and the Earl of Northumberland, by which they agreed to divide the whole kingdom of England and Wales between them. Then the English gradually reasserted control, and by 1409 Owain seems to have been a fugitive; his death is not recorded, and probably did not happen until about 1415.

These events concern the question of who rules the country, and how completely he is able to control it – the history of monarchs and battles. But of course politics is about more than that: in fifteenth-century England it was very much about religion as well. There was enough wrong with the church to cause a great deal of discontent: priests often ignored their vow of chastity, and higher church officials, regarding their office mainly as a source of income, might be non-resident, perhaps not even living in England, so that church revenues might be drained out of the country; and since the church was ruled from Rome, it was virtually impossible for its abuses in England to be reformed. Since the services were in Latin, and there was no English bible, ordinary people were inevitably cut off from a religion that nonetheless ruled their lives.

Pressure for reform built up during the fourteenth century, the main reformer being John Wycliff, who died in 1387; his followers, known as Lollards, grew more and more active, and during the reign of Henry they were fiercely persecuted. Religious toleration, allowing everyone to hold their own beliefs and to worship how and where they wished, which is now universal in Christendom, was still more or less unknown. There were many Lollard martyrs in fifteenth-century England: one was Sir John Oldcastle, condemned for heresy and savagely killed in 1417.

3

The king's troubles continued, and included open disagreements with his son over policy. In 1411 he succeeded in removing the prince from the Council, but he was a sick man, and died in 1413. His son became Henry V, waged successful military campaigns in France, married the French princess, and managed to get himself declared heir to the French throne, but died there in 1422. He was succeeded by his infant son, whose long reign as Henry VI was a time of constant trouble and civil war. The struggle between the houses of York and Lancaster, descended from two of the sons of Edward III, is known as the Wars of the Roses – possibly the worst civil strife in English history. Henry was deposed in 1460, and succeeded by Edward Duke of York, who reigned as Edward IV; when he died in 1485 he left two young sons, but the crown fell to his brother Richard, who ruled as Richard III for three years, during which the young princes were kept in the Tower of London, where they died mysteriously. Richard's enemies, of whom there were many, believed he had murdered them.

Meanwhile a Welsh nobleman called Henry Tudor had managed to construct a very plausible claim to the throne, and after defeating Richard's army at the battle of Bosworth in 1485, he was crowned as Henry VII. That marked the end of the Wars of the Roses, and the beginning of the Tudor dynasty, which lasted until the death of Queen Elizabeth in 1603.

All this was well known in the sixteenth century: historians and poets published accounts of the Plantagenet kings, and in particular of the civil strife between the houses of York and Lancaster that culminated in the terrible Wars of the Roses, and eventually in the establishment of the Tudors on the throne in 1485. During the reign of Henry VIII several historians wrote accounts of the previous turbulent century, usually with the purpose of praising the achievement of Henry's father in putting an end to civil strife and uniting the two houses of Lancaster and York. Thus an Italian called Polydore Vergil began writing a history of England at the request of King Henry VII, which was published and partly translated in the time of Henry VIII; and Sir Thomas More wrote an (unfinished) life of Richard III. Most important was *The Union of the Noble And Illustre Families of Lancastre and York* (1542) by Edward Hall, which puts forward a providential view of English history, tracing God's plan behind the alternations of good and bad kings. Hall's main purpose is to celebrate the achievements of Henry VIII, in whose reign he was writing, and to whom he devotes half of his book; and he precedes his account of Henry's reign with an account of the fifteenth century, from Henry IV 'the beginning and root of the great discord and division', to the 'godly matrimony' of Henry VII that was, as he optimistically declares, 'the final end of all dissensions titles and debates'.

This view of English history has obvious political implications, as the study of history always had in the sixteenth century. Kings were thought to hold their authority from God, and the threefold analogy between God, king, and father was a commonplace: God is king of the universe and father of mankind, the king is father of his people and rules with divine authority, the father is king of the household and a God to his family. The 1547 Book of Homilies required preachers to remind their congregations of the need to obey the monarch and the wickedness of rebellion, and the civil strife of the fifteenth century was constantly described in terms that emphasised the need for obedience and the holiness of royal authority. The extreme version of this was the doctrine of the Divine Right of Kings, which had originally been formulated in the Holy Roman Empire as a weapon against the Papacy (the emperor held his authority direct from God, and not through the intermediary of the Pope), and which became more and more prominent in England under the Tudors and the Stuarts.

It is not certain how much of Hall and other historians of the early sixteenth-century Shakespeare read, but he certainly knew several works on English history published during the reign of Elizabeth. Most important of these is Raphael Holinshed's *History of England,* which appeared in 1577, and was reprinted ten years later, along with histories of Ireland and Scotland, and a *Description of England,* all by other writers. Holinshed is a rather pedestrian historian, but the fact that Shakespeare used him as his main source has earned him a posthumous fame. He begins his account of Henry IV with firm disapproval of his usurpation, but as the narrative continues and the troubles caused by the rebellion of the Percys grow more and more evident, the disapproval tends to shift towards the rebels. Since modern scholarly editions of *Henry IV*, such as the Arden Shakespeare, reprint extracts from Holinshed, it is not difficult for readers to compare Shakespeare's main source with what he did to it.

Two other works published in the later sixteenth-century were certainly used by Shakespeare. In 1580 John Stow published *The Chronicles of England*: this is chiefly relevant to us for its account of the young prince's wild youth, which is discussed below, see p. 21; and in 1595 Samuel Daniel published a long poem about 'the civil wars between the two houses of Lancaster and York'. Daniel was an accomplished lyrical poet, but this attempt at historical narrative is a pedestrian work, full of moralising, and sometimes vague on details. Like Holinshed, it is remembered chiefly because Shakespeare read it, and drew on it for one or two facts. Its account of how Henry IV gained the throne is very hostile, referring to the 'sin of usurpation' and the 'greater crime' of the murder of Richard, but Daniel, like Holinshed, grows more sympathetic to Henry in his later years. Perhaps the most interesting section, for the reader of Shakespeare, is its account of the battle of Shrewsbury, which describes the Prince of Wales as 'that new appearing glorious star, | Wonder of arms, the terror of the field' and mentions the help he gave to his 'indangered father', but it has more to say about the king's bravery than his son's. It treats Hotspur as brave but wrong:

> What ark, what trophy, what magnificence
> Of glory, Hotspur, hadst thou purchased here;
> Could but thy cause, as fair as thy pretence,
> Be made unto thy country to appear

and it tells us that only Hotspur's death prevented the king's party from losing even more of his supporters. We are not told who killed Hotspur, who 'fighting dies, and dying kills withal'. The poem deals at some length with Henry's death, including the episode of the crown, which the son removes from his father's bed while he is asleep, resulting first in a reproach from the king and then an explanation, forgiveness and dying advice.

And then, a year or two after Daniel's poem, the leading dramatist of the company known as the Lord Chamberlain's Men turned, for the second time, to English history for his subject.

2

Shakespeare's *Henry IV*

Shakespeare wrote ten plays about English history: two tetralogies (sets of four connected plays) and two individual plays (*King John* and *Henry VIII*) which need not concern us here. The term 'tetralogy' should not be taken too seriously: it is a convenient way of referring to the fact that the four plays tell a continuous story, but need not imply that they were planned as a unity; how far this is the case with *Henry IV* is discussed later. The first tetralogy, comprising the three parts of *Henry VI* and *Richard III*, was probably written by 1592, and deals with the civil wars of the mid-fifteenth century, culminating in the death of Richard and the crowning of Henry VII. It is among Shakespeare's earliest work: the blank verse is rather stiffly regular, and the construction rather mechanical, but it can be very powerful on stage, especially in its depiction of the horrors of civil war. The last of the four plays, *Richard III*, is certainly the most successful, and is the most often performed. Its depiction of Richard as a total villain, depraved and pleased with his own depravity, power-hungry in a way that is both frightening and comic, is theatrically very effective, and has attracted great actors to the part. Both this view of Richard and the portrayal of Henry (known in the play as Richmond) as a great white hero who rescues England from Richard's tyranny, belong clearly in the official Tudor view of English history,

Five or six years later (probably in 1596) Shakespeare returned to English history, and began another tetralogy, moving back in time to the reigns of Richard II, Henry IV and Henry V. Now at the height of his powers, he gives a richer and more complex picture of English society, in verse that is much more supple and complex. The first of these plays deals with the deposition of

Richard II, who is depicted as sensitive, temperamental and irresponsible, a bad ruler but an eloquent orator, more suited to the role of court poet than king. The play opens with a quarrel between his cousin, Henry Bolingbroke, and Thomas Mowbray, Duke of Norfolk, both of whom appear to know something to the king's discredit that is never fully explained. The king settles the matter by banishing them both, and then when John of Gaunt, Bolingbroke's father, dies, seizes his estates to finance his Irish wars. Bolingbroke then defies the sentence of banishment, and returns with an army, claiming 'I come but for my own', but succeeds in deposing Richard, and becomes King Henry IV. Richard is imprisoned in Pomfret Castle, where, with Bolingbroke's connivance, he is murdered.

The deposing of Richard is of course the main theme of the play, and the contrast between the two kings is central. Richard is eloquent, self-regarding and pathetic; Bolingbroke is competent and practical and knows when to keep in the background. The crucial encounter with Richard at Flint castle, when he is taken prisoner, is entrusted to the Earl of Northumberland, at whom Richard directs his reproaches and his insistence on the Divine Right of Kings. Northumberland is still in charge during the scene in which Richard is compelled to resign the crown, and in which his eloquent, self-pitying play-acting contrasts with the calm brevity of Bolingbroke declaring 'In God's name, I'll ascend the royal throne.' Bolingbroke is all quiet strength where Richard is all eloquent weakness.

Only at the very end of the play do we glimpse a different Bolingbroke. Richard is killed by Exton, acting on Bolingbroke's words 'Have I no friend will rid me of this living fear?', and no doubt hoping for reward; but Bolingbroke, when the news is brought to him, declares 'They love not poison that do poison need', and banishes Exton from his sight. He then declares publicly 'my soul is full of woe', and announces his intention to go on a pilgrimage to the Holy Land.

When the next play opens, some time has passed. Bolingbroke – now King Henry IV – is not the quiet man of action we saw in *Richard II*: he announces in the very first line of the play that he is 'shaken' and 'wan with care', and has turned into the beleaguered and sleepless figure whose right to rule is being constantly challenged. At the end of *Richard II* Bolingbroke

8

announced his wish to lead a crusade to the Holy Land, and this is now caught up and expanded:

> Therefore friends,
> As far as to the sepulchre of Christ –
> Whose soldier now, under whose blessed cross
> We are impresséd and engaged to fight –
> Forthwith a power of English shall we levy,
> Whose arms were moulded in their mother's womb
> To chase these pagans in those holy fields
> Over whose acres walked those blesséd feet,
> Which fourteen hundred years ago were nailed
> For our advantage on the bitter cross

(1HIV: I. i. 18)

Two comments need making on this passage. The first is specific to Henry. The real Henry had in fact been to Jerusalem, as a young man in 1392–3, but this is never mentioned in the play: perhaps the urge to lead a crusade seems more powerful if it is felt to be a new experience. The second concerns the nature of crusades. Perhaps theory and practice have seldom been so far apart as in this series of episodes, which ostensibly had a purely devotional purpose, to gain access to the holy places of Jerusalem, but in practice were often purely military expeditions, attacking Muslim states and – very often – other Christian powers: fellow crusaders, and, on one scandalous occasion, Byzantium. The first and most successful Crusade began in 1096, and the ensuing century was the great epoch of crusading; by the time of Henry Bolingbroke the Crusades belonged to the past. But one of the striking features of the crusading ideal was how long it outlasted the reality: the wish to make a pious journey, even a pious military journey, to the Holy Land was alive long after such journeys were no longer likely to happen. Henry's crusading wish is presented in this play in terms of piety, not at all as a wish for conquest or riches, so that though these lines begin by apparently describing a war of conquest, we can see their spirit changing as they proceed. The line 'To chase the pagans in those holy fields' marks the transition: the first four lines are warlike, the last three describe and dwell on the 'holy fields'. It's as if the Crusade is first described in appropriately military terms but then turns into a purely devotional act. Finally, we are told that the project has to be

9

postponed because of political pressures at home, and we hear no more about it until the end of Act IV in the second play, when Henry asks the name of the room in his palace in which he is about to die. Told that it is called 'Jerusalem', he reflects sadly on the prophecy that he should die in Jerusalem, 'which vainly I supposed the Holy Land.' By now, crusading has lost all its military meaning, and is seen as a pure act of devotion: no longer something performed in the real world, but more like a pious wish.

Henry IV, then, begins with the longing to set out on a crusade because it is clear that the king is in trouble at home. From Wales has come the news that Edmund Mortimer has been defeated and captured by 'the irregular and wild Glendower'. From Scotland the news at first seemed better – young Hotspur has defeated the rebel Douglas and taken a lot of Scottish prisoners: but this news is soured by his refusal to yield up his prisoners to the king. Most serious of all is the fact that the Percy family, who helped him to the throne, has begun to turn against him. Since the Percys dominate the first act, we can begin with them.

THE REBELS

We meet three Percys. The dominant one appears to be Worcester, brother of the Earl of Northumberland. He it is whom the king appears to consider the dangerous one ('Worcester, get thee gone, for I do see | Danger and disobedience in thine eye'), and he is the one who seems in charge of the family council. He too it is who later decides not to tell his nephew of the king's offer, before the battle, of a peaceful settlement. Northumberland, in contrast, who had run Bolingbroke's campaign with such cool ruthlessness in the previous play, now remains on the fringe of the action. He does not appear at the decisive battle at Shrewsbury, sending a message that he is sick, and we are left unsure just how genuine this sickness is. There are clues both ways: the messenger who brings the news tells us that he was 'much-feared by his physicians', but Rumour, the chorus who introduces Part 2, speaks of his being 'crafty-sick'. When the news of his son's death emerges from the rumours, he suddenly finds himself cured:

> In poison there is physic, and these news,
> Having been well, that would have made me sick,
> Being sick, have in some measure made me well.
>
> (2HIV: I. i. 137)

This moment can be very effective theatrically, as he throws aside his stick or his nightcap or suddenly stands up, and it could be interpreted either as confirming that the sickness was feigned or at least psychosomatic, or else as a glimpse of the incomprehensible relation of mind and body. It is surely meant to be remembered by the attentive listener when the exact opposite happens to the king in Act IV, Scene iv. Westmorland brings news of the tricking of Archbishop Scrope, which the king greets with two lyrical lines

> O Westmorland, thou art a summer bird,
> Which ever in the haunch of winter sings
> The lifting up of day;
>
> (IV. iv. 91)   -

Then Harcourt brings news of the defeat of Northumberland (at Bramham Moor). These two victories (which were actually three years apart) are coupled to suggest a decisive success for the king's forces, and also to invert what happened to Northumberland. The king's reaction to Harcourt's news is:

> And wherefore should these good news make me sick?
>   . . . . .
> I should rejoice now at this happy news,
> And now my sight fails, and my brain is giddy
>
> (IV. iv. 102)

– and he does not recover. Once again we are offered a glimpse of the puzzling relation of mind and body: that bad news can make us well, good news can make us ill. This is strikingly similar to Freud's account of 'those wrecked by success'. In a paper entitled 'Some Character-types met with in Psycho-analytic Work' (1915) Freud claimed 'that people occasionally fall ill precisely because a deeply-rooted and long-cherished wish has come to fulfilment'. He actually illustrates this syndrome from Shakespeare, citing Lady Macbeth as an example, but Henry IV would have served as well, with the added fascination provided by the contrasting case of Northumberland.

We get one further glimpse of Northumberland, and once again it explores his hesitation between action and inaction. Act II, Scene iii opens with Northumberland declaring that he is setting off for war because his 'honour is at pawn'; his wife and – much more passionately – his now widowed daughter-in-law beg him not to go: she contrasts the need to redeem his honour now with the far greater need there had been to support his son at Shrewsbury:

> Never, O never, do his ghost the wrong
> To hold your honour more precise and nice
> With others than with him!

(II. iii. 39)

She does not actually say that he had been quite capable of going to Shrewsbury; that interpretation is left to us. Northumberland finally decides to go to Scotland instead of joining the rebellion, perhaps an uneasy compromise that gets the worst of both worlds. He is a very different character from the calmly efficient man of action we saw in *Richard II* – and perhaps a more interesting one.

But by far the most interesting of the rebels, and for many the most attractive character in the play, is Percy's son Henry, known as Hotspur. Whereas Prince Hal (as we shall see) is two-faced, Hotspur is all of a piece: hot-tempered, brave, defiant and attractively impulsive. We first meet him defying the king about his Scottish prisoners. According to the laws of chivalry, he was obliged to yield up to the king all prisoners of royal blood, and by yielding Mordrake Earl of Fife he is presumably obeying this rule, and putting himself technically in the right. Whether he is legally entitled to keep the rest is never made clear, and it is soon obvious that it's not the legality of keeping them that is in question, but his insistence on his own honour. Hotspur will not give way to anyone he does not respect, and clearly despises the foppish messenger, 'perfumèd like a milliner', who came to demand the prisoners on the field of battle, and whom he so vividly and contemptuously describes. Shakespeare often brings main characters in front of us rather gradually, but Hotspur reveals himself fully from the beginning:

> My liege, I did deny no prisoners.
> But I remember when the fight was done,
> When I was dry with rage and extreme toil,
> Breathless and faint, leaning upon my sword,
> Came there a certain lord, neat and trimly dressed,
> Fresh as a bridegroom, and his chin new reaped
> Showed like a stubble land at harvest home

(1HIV: I. iii. 28)

Hotspur's self-presentation is vivid and immediate: he is a fighter, at home on the battlefield, moved to irritation by the inappropriate elegance of the courtier with perfume and designer stubble. This breaking of decorum is far more vivid to us, and more important to Hotspur, than the question at issue, so that he never actually says whether or not he is now prepared to hand over the prisoners (we soon learn that he doesn't). From this first moment we know Hotspur: hot-tempered, vividly eloquent, and so concerned with his own dignity that he does not even notice that he is evading the question. Hotspur is the dominant character in this scene (I, iii), and we are shown the changes he can ring on register, all revealing of his character. The king's dismissive reference to 'revolted Mortimer' prompts an indignant account of the combat between Mortimer and Glendower in rather stiff and old-fashioned rhetoric:

> He did confound the best part of an hour
> In changing hardiment with great Glendower.
> . . . . .
> Never did bare and rotten policy
> Colour her working with such deadly wounds

(I. iii. 99)

There is very little rhyme in this play, and Hotspur seems to drop into rhyme as a way of signalling that he is going to make a set speech, designed to show that Mortimer was, as we might put it today, a good chap. The king's response, that this combat never took place, is probably correct (there is no reference to such a combat in the sources, or elsewhere in the play), but that is unimportant: the speech is there for rhetorical effect. The

13

reference to 'bare and rotten policy' – in contrast to bravery in battle – seems arbitrary at first, but we soon learn that it is a reference to the king: to 'this vile politician Bolingbroke'. 'Policy', in sixteenth-century usage, could mean trickery or underhand dealings, and a 'politician' a trickster, dishonest and untrustworthy; and referring to the king by the title he had before he became king is a subtle way of dethroning him.

Hotspur's impulsiveness is very clearly contrasted with his uncle's scheming; and we see this again before the battle. When Sir Walter Blunt comes to parley in Act IV, Scene iii, requiring to know the nature of the rebels' demands, Hotspur responds by reciting his version of Bolingbroke's rise to power, as if it is necessary for him to get this off his chest before he can attend to the question; then when Blunt asks, no doubt impatiently, 'Shall I return this answer to the king?' Hotspur can pay attention, and replies quite reasonably that they will confer and then reply. Worcester, in contrast, who never loses his temper, is capable of considered deception, and decides to conceal the king's offer of a peaceful settlement:

> It is not possible, it cannot be,
> The King should keep his word in loving us.
> He will suspect us still, and find a time
> To punish this offence in other faults.

> (V. ii. 4)

Worcester speaks like a follower of Machiavelli, offering a cynical but realistic assessment of the situation: one that Hotspur would be incapable of making.

Two corollaries of Hotspur's military nature are shown us. One is his handling of women. In Act II, Scene iii of Part 1 his wife pleads with him to take her into his confidence:

> Some heavy business hath my lord in hand,
> And I must know it, else he loves me not.

> (II. iii. 65)

But he refuses to do so, goes out of his way to show more interest in his horse than in her, and puts her off with 'Away, you trifler! Love! I love thee not.'

Two or three years after writing this scene, Shakespeare wrote another and very different version of a wife begging to be

14

taken into her husband's confidence. Portia, wife of Brutus in *Julius Caesar*, reproaches her husband in similar terms to Kate, but receives a very different reply. Brutus at first evades her questioning, but when she insists that if she is told none of his secrets then 'Portia is Brutus' harlot, not his wife' he yields: 'O ye gods, | Render me worthy of this noble wife!'

On one level, this comparison is clearly in favour of Brutus: Portia would certainly feel that Hotspur treats Kate as his harlot not his wife. But this remark reminds us that the Hotspur–Kate scene can be played with an erotic charge quite absent from the dignified, almost prim exchange between Brutus and Portia. Their scene needs to be played with restraint and some formality, whereas that between Hotspur and Kate is usually, on the modern stage, played as a love scene, even a romp. 'Out, you mad-headed ape,' she says to him; and 'In faith, I'll break thy little finger, Harry' as she struggles with him in a blend – surely – of frustration and sexual attraction. Of course this is more easily done on the modern stage, where Kate is played by a woman, than it can have been with Elizabethan boy actors playing the female parts. It is often remarked that love scenes in the Elizabethan theatre include very little physical contact, simply because that would be inappropriate with boys playing the female roles. This is often but by no means always true: the later scene with Mortimer and his wife includes some very explicit sexuality, as well as sexual banter between Hotspur and Kate. If we were offered a time machine to watch Shakespeare's company performing a scene, perhaps Hotspur and Kate would be the one to choose.

Also striking in Hotspur is an impulsiveness that can be seen as either childish or attractively spontaneous – or indeed as both. The conference with Glendower and Mortimer (III. i) shows Shakespeare at his most brilliant in depicting changes and contrasts of mood. It has a certain basis in fact, since Mortimer, Glendower and the Percys did agree on an alliance, but virtually every detail in Shakespeare's version is fictitious. He made it a meeting between the three principals, not just their representatives, set it at Glendower's house so that it could be combined with the domestic scene which follows, and used it to show the contrast between Hotspur's youthful impatience, sexual banter and concern for his own reputation on the one hand, and Glendower's rather pompous dignity on the other.

> GLEN. I can call spirits from the vasty deep.
> HOT. Why so can I, or so can any man:
>   But will they come when you do call for them?

(III. i. 50)

It is the sturdy common sense of the Englishman set against Welsh mumbo-jumbo – as Hotspur explains at some length when describing how Glendower kept him up 'at least nine hours | In reckoning up the several devils' names', along with 'such a deal of skimble-skamble stuff'. Hotspur's mockery of all this magic is more entertaining than Glendower's solemn invocations, and also more linguistically inventive: we cannot imagine Glendower coining words like 'skimble-skamble' (which Shakespeare seems to have invented).

Hotspur is not exactly stirring up racial hatred, but in this age of racial sensitivity, we cannot fail to notice his narrowness. His dismissal of Glendower has about it something of the blunt Englishman's dismissal of anything foreign, as if the Welsh language itself is contemptible: 'Let me not understand you then: speak it in Welsh.' This prompts Glendower's surely rather dignified reply: 'I can speak English, lord, as well as you.' Neither Worcester nor Mortimer is as lively or as entertaining as Hotspur, but their reproaches to him do tell him – and us – that Glendower holds him 'in high respect', though Hotspur has been putting him 'quite besides his patience'. In the division of the kingdom we have just seen Hotspur's petulance over geography itself, complaining that the course of the Trent deprives him of 'a huge half-moon, a monstrous cantle there', and Glendower's equally obstinate reply. It looks like an impasse, until Glendower gives way with a shrug, and Hotspur shrugs too, revealing that they were only two schoolboys daring each other over nothing.

The third member of the alliance, Edmund Mortimer, involves a mistake on Shakespeare's part (based on the same mistake in Holinshed). The Edmund Mortimer who surrendered to Glendower and then married his daughter was not actually a claimant to the throne. He was the younger brother of Roger Mortimer, Earl of March, great-grandson of Edward III, who after the death of Richard had the most authentic claim to the succession, and had actually been named by Richard as the rightful successor. Roger was dead by the time this scene takes place, and his son Edmund has been confused with the Edmund who was actually his uncle.

But entertaining as this conference scene is, it is also serious politics. What we are seeing is the alliance preparing to divide England into three parts, and the colourful details (Hotspur's petulant complaint that the river Trent cuts off a big piece of his share) should not distract our attention from realising that these rebels are treating England not as a kingdom to be governed, but as booty to be divided. A few years later, in *King Lear*, Shakespeare wrote another scene in which the country is divided into three parts, and that division of the kingdom was evidence of Lear's folly, and the beginning of moral and political chaos. Kingdoms should be left intact.

THE TWO HARRYS

1 Henry IV is built on the contrast between the Prince of Wales and Hotspur. The decision to do this was Shakespeare's own, and to achieve it he had to take liberties with the facts. It is true that the King's son and Percy's son were both called Henry (after their fathers) – and Henry can of course be abbreviated to either Harry or Hal – but they were very different in age: Hotspur was 38 at the time this play begins, and Prince Hal 15. The contrast between him and Hal is announced from the beginning, as the king ruefully contemplates the difference between the two:

> O that it could be proved
> That some night-tripping fairy had exchanged
> In cradle clothes our children where they lay,
> And called mine Percy, his Plantagenet!
> Then would I have his Harry, and he mine.

(I. i. 85)

This speech of the king's announces what is really the central theme of the play, the contrast between the two Harrys; and to achieve this it was necessary not only to take liberties with their ages, but to readjust the treatment of the politics. The rebellion of the Percys and that of the Welsh were both serious dangers to

17

Henry's position, but they followed very different courses: the Welsh uprising was protracted, fought by guerrilla tactics and refusal of taxation, and was only gradually overcome, whereas the Percy rebellion was put down in three decisive encounters, the battle of Shrewsbury in 1403, the encounter at Gaultree in 1405, and the battle of Bramham Moor in 1408. Only the first of these comes in Part 1, of which it forms the climax. The battle itself is historical: the Percys were defeated by the king's forces at Shrewsbury in 1403, and both Hotspur and his uncle Worcester were killed there. But Prince Hal, though he may have been present, did not play a prominent part, and he did not meet Percy in single combat. Holinshed has more to say about the king's bravery than his son's, and tells us that the king 'did that day many a noble feat of arms, for as it is written, he slew that day with his own hands six and thirty persons of his enemies. The other on his part encouraged by his doings fought valiantly, and slew the lord Percy, called sir Henry Hotspur.' *The other* here means 'the rest' (we would now say 'the others', but this use of the singular was normal in the sixteenth century), but if hastily read it could be taken to refer to the prince, who was mentioned a few lines earlier. Some scholars have therefore suggested that Holinshed's sentence was misread by Shakespeare, leading him to believe – or perhaps just suggesting the possibility to him – that the prince killed Hotspur.

But there is no need to hunt for a textual basis in Holinshed. A victorious battle makes a far more effective climax for a play than a gradual war of attrition, so it was more or less inevitable that Shakespeare should push Glendower into the background – a passing remark by the king in the very last scene announces that he and his son will move into Wales 'to fight with Glendower and the Earl of March' – and make the battle of Shrewsbury the climax of the play, and the encounter of the two Harrys the climax of that battle. By making the contrast between them so central, while at the same time keeping them apart, he built up to a climax so intense that it has no need of verbal elaboration. When Hal and Hotspur meet for the first time on the battlefield their exchange is, on the surface, very straightforward:

> HOT. If I mistake not, thou art Harry Monmouth.
> HAL. Thou speakest as if I would deny my name.

HOT. My name is Harry Percy.
HAL.   Why then I see
    A very valiant rebel of the name.
    I am the Prince of Wales, and think not, Percy,
    To share with me in glory any more.
    Two stars keep not their motion in one sphere,
    Nor can one England brook a double reign
    Of Harry Percy and the Prince of Wales.

(v. iv. 58)

The whole play is contained in these deceptively simple lines. The 'names' which are so central to the exchange are imbued with significance. Hal has in one sense 'denied his name' all through the play because of his wild and unprincely behaviour, but at this climax he has the chance to assert who he is. Hotspur puts together the two names – Harry Percy, Harry Monmouth – making them sound exactly equal, balancing the syllables against each other in a way which allows no decoration, no pulling of rank. Hal both accepts and rejects this equality: he pays Percy the compliment of treating him as an equal while at the same time reminding him that he is not (so though he is 'very valiant', he is just 'a very valiant rebel'). The most important – and in a good production the most moving – line in this exchange is the last one quoted: 'Of Harry Percy and the Prince of Wales': it contains no verbal ingenuity, but simply, by its plain juxtaposition, allows the two names to resonate against each other, and asserts the whole theme of the play. Historical untruth seems a small price to pay for such dramatic power.

But there is a complication, which we need to discuss when we come to Falstaff.

THE REBELS IN PART 2

When we come to Part 2 England is still torn by civil strife, but all the previous leaders except Northumberland have disappeared; and Northumberland, elderly and ill, hesitant and even dithering, is never seen as a possible candidate for the heroic treatment that was given to his son. In historical fact, the rebels were defeated twice: by a stratagem at Gaultree forest in 1405, where they were led by Scrope, the archbishop of York and the

Earl of Mowbray; and in battle at Bramham Moor in 1408, led by the Earl of Northumberland, who was there killed. Clearly Shakespeare could have chosen Bramham Moor as the climax, and so ended Part 2, like Part 1, with a victory in battle for the king's party; clearly, too, with no Hotspur, this would have given us a pale echo of the ending of Part 1. So Bramham Moor is not even named, and this final defeat of the rebels is given only a brief mention at Act IV, Scene iv, 97, where it seems to take place at much the same time as Gaultree. It is the stratagem, not the battle, that is given extended treatment, in the first three scenes of Act IV.

The rebels are led now by the archbishop of York, 'whose white investments figure innocence'. The fact that they are led by a priest is significant, and is mentioned several times in the text, not only by Westmorland, the king's representative, but also by the archbishop himself ('Nor do I as an enemy to peace Troop in the throngs of military men'). Prince John of Lancaster makes it the occasion of a lengthy rebuke:

> My Lord of York, it better showed with you
> When that your flock, assembled by the bell,
> Encircled you to hear with reverence
> Your exposition on the holy text
> Than now to see you here, an iron man
>
> (IV. ii. 4)

A rebellion led by an archbishop could produce either of two opposite effects on a sixteenth-century audience: either that the cause must be good and the incentive strong if it has led a priest to take arms, or that priests, of all people, ought not to meddle in politics and cause civil strife. The more hard-headed and anti-clerical the spectator, the more likely is the second response. In production, the archbishop could be dressed either in his priestly robes or in armour to make the point, and both have been tried on the modern stage. Logically, one could put up an equally strong case for either, but if we remember that drama is visual as well as verbal, the case for dressing him like a priest seems to me overwhelming, since the inappropriateness would then be constantly in front of our eyes.

The rebels present a list of complaints that is kept vague, so that we never learn what exactly their rebellion is trying to achieve. The trick used to defeat them – promising to rectify their grievances but not promising to pardon them – could be seen as showing either the naivety of the rebels or the low cunning of the king's party: modern commentators have tended to emphasise the element of trickery and to view it is a kind of medieval sleaze, but an Elizabethan audience, aware of the dangers of armed rebellion, are likely to have responded with mixed feelings: no doubt it produced lively arguments among the spectators when the show was over. The negotiation is conducted by Prince John of Lancaster, second son of the king, assisted by the Earl of Westmorland: this serves to distance both the king and the Prince of Wales from the trickery. But since in historical fact it was conducted by Westmorland alone, it would have been possible for Shakespeare to have removed the royal family completely from the picture, and he must have chosen not to.

Of course there is another reason for not ending Part 2 with a victorious battle: Shakespeare clearly had other plans for the climax.

HAL'S WILD YOUTH

Shakespeare did not invent the story of the prince's dissolute youth, but he certainly treated it with unprecedented fullness, and indeed made it as prominent as the main story: there are more or less the same number of lines in the Hal/Falstaff scenes and the court scenes. We do not know much about the historical Prince Henry's behaviour as a young man, but the suggestions that it was wild seem to go back almost (perhaps not quite) to his own time. Shakespeare would have found details about it in almost all the sources he consulted. John Stowe's *Annals of England* (1592) tells how he sometimes waited for his own receivers (that is, tax-collectors) and robbed them – and then paid them back! – and several sources record the quarrel with the Lord Chief Justice, who is said to have imprisoned one of the prince's followers. The tradition of the Prince's youthful dissipation was especially strong in the theatre, as we can see from the anonymous play called *The Famous Victories of Henry the Fifth*, published in 1598, but almost certainly written before

21

Shakespeare's tetralogies. Perhaps the best way to look at Shakespeare's treatment of the theme will be to start with this play.

It begins, as do Shakespeare's Eastcheap scenes, with travellers being ambushed and robbed, though in *The Famous Victories* Hal takes part in the robbery, whereas in Shakespeare he and Poins keep out of it in order to play a trick on Falstaff. In the third scene of *The Famous Victories* the king reproaches the lord mayor of London for committing his son to prison; and in reply the mayor describes the street brawl caused by the prince and his followers, and his uncertainty as to whether they had been sent by the king to test him. We then move to court, where the Lord Chief Justice is trying a character simply called 'Thief'; the prince arrives, sees that the prisoner is his servant, and protests; when the judge will not give way, the prince gives him a box on the ear, and is hauled off to prison. In the next scene the prince and two of his men are discussing what has happened, and the prince promises 'Ned' that when he is king 'thou shalt be my Lord Chief Justice'. The prince is then summoned to his father, where after a short speech of repentance he is reconciled and forgiven, though they seem for a moment about to quarrel again when the prince, thinking his father dead, removes the crown from his pillow, but he justifies his action and they are reconciled once again as the king dies. Now that Henry V is king he makes it clear that he going to give up his former life and companions.

Although this play was not published until 1598 (that is, after Shakespeare had written his two *Henry IV* plays), it must have existed and been performed earlier, and there is no doubt that Shakespeare knew it and drew on it. He no doubt saw it performed, and may well have had access to the written text. The robbery at Gadshill, the quarrel and reconciliation with the Lord Chief Justice, the reconciliation with his father, including the episode of the prince taking and returning the crown, and the final banishing of his followers, are all there, even with a few verbal parallels, such as the command that the followers are not to come near his person 'by ten mile'. There are striking parallels, too, between the later scenes of this play and Shakespeare's *Henry V*, such as the mocking gift of tennis balls from the French Dauphin to Henry.

So like and so unlike: the comparison between *The Famous Victories* and *Henry IV* is an object lesson in the usefulness of looking at Shakespeare's sources, for the old play has nothing of the quality which makes Shakespeare's work such a master-piece. (I should add that the text we have may well be a shortened and simplified version of what was performed, but we have no evidence of what was left out.) Every episode is minimal and crude, and the main value of the comparison is to show us how Shakespeare can turn lead into gold. The prince joins in the robbery wholeheartedly in the old play; in Shakespeare he is detached from it, so that we are never sure whether his purpose is to participate or to use it to play a trick on his followers. Similarly, in the reconciliation with his father the old play moves us from a callous eagerness to succeed ('I stand upon thorns till the crown be on my head') to a sudden and crude repentance ('My conscience accuseth me . . . Ah Harry now, thrice unhappy Harry'); Shakespeare's prince is a much more complex and even mysterious figure, whom we now need to look at.

The original audience of Shakespeare's play probably knew that Hal had been a rake in youth, and had reformed to become England's hero-king; and since they knew it, and the dramatist could not pretend to offer them a surprise, they might as well be reminded from the beginning:

> I know you all, and will awhile uphold
> The unyoked humour of your idleness.
> Yet herein will I imitate the sun,
> Who doth permit the base contagious clouds
> To smother up his beauty from the world,
> That when he please again to be himself,
> Being wanted, he may be more wondered at
> By breaking through the foul and ugly mists
> Of vapours that did seem to strangle him.
> If all the year were playing holidays,
> To sport would be as tedious as to work;
> But when they seldom come, they wished-for come,
> And nothing pleaseth but rare accidents.
> So when this loose behaviour I throw off,
> And pay the debt I never promised,
> By how much better than my word I am,
> By so much shall I falsify men's hopes.

And like bright metal on a sullen ground,
My reformation, glittering o'er my fault,
Shall show more goodly and attract more eyes
Than that which hath no foil to set it off.
I'll so offend, to make offence a skill,
Redeeming time when men think least I will.

(I. ii. 193)

That is Prince Hal's soliloquy at the end of his first scene with his followers, in which he announces the change that will come over him when he becomes king, ten acts later. It offers the audience a framework for our enjoyment of the comic scenes, a reminder that the prince does not altogether belong there. The speech, in other words, can be seen as a kind of chorus, and in delivering it the prince is commenting on his own behaviour – like Desdemona, joking with Iago, and adding 'I am not merry, but I do beguile | The thing I am by seeming otherwise.' Such an effect is not possible in wholly naturalistic drama, in which whatever a character says needs to be what he would plausibly say in that situation; but the very fact that a play is in verse, or that a character speaks a soliloquy, is a reminder that the represented world is not a purely naturalistic one.

Yet everything is complex in Shakespeare. It would, after all, have been possible to bring a chorus onto the stage to inform us directly that Hal is going to reform: Elizabethan dramatists sometimes used choruses, though not usually – for obvious reasons – to tell us what is going to happen. Shakespeare was not fond of the device, but two of the rare occasions that he did use it are in the two following plays of the tetralogy, 2 Henry IV and Henry V. It would appear that he here preferred the effect of making Hal step out of the action in order to deliver this partly choric comment, and in the hands of a good actor the effect of detaching himself from his comrades in order to say 'I know you all', as if speaking both to them as they depart and also to the audience, can be very powerful. It faces us with the question of just what the prince is up to, in the way an ordinary chorus might not.

And what is he up to? He is sometimes, for instance, compared to Haroun-al-Raschid, the caliph of Baghdad, who in the Arabian Nights wandered about the city in disguise in order to get to know his people. Will not Hal, as critics have often suggested, make a better king because of the way he has got to know his subjects? When, as king, he wanders through the camp in disguise on the night before Agincourt, cheering his soldiers, offering them 'a little touch of Harry in the night', is he not drawing on what he learned in Eastcheap?

Perhaps he is; but that was not his motive. This opening soliloquy is entirely concerned with the contrast between what people expect from him and what they are going to get, that is, with his own reputation, not with learning to know and love his subjects, and so become a better king. We can see this in the episode with Francis. At the beginning of Act II, Scene iv, the prince confides to Poins that he has 'sounded the very base-string of humility': he has been talking to the drawers (the waiters), is now their sworn brother and 'can call them all by their Christian names', so that 'when I am king of England I shall command all the good lads of Eastcheap'. He then arranges with Poins to call Francis, the drawer, from the next room while the prince is talking to him, so that the unfortunate Francis is pulled in two directions and has to keep calling out 'anon' (soon) while the prince keeps putting fresh questions to him, so that the poor lad doesn't know which way to turn. It is a piece of crude comedy, no doubt effective on the stage if well acted, but in our democratic age it is difficult for an audience not to sympathise with Francis and think that the prince is using his rank to torment someone who cannot answer back; and even by Elizabethan standards it is clear that the social distance is more important than any feeling of common humanity.

Perhaps nothing is more important, in thinking about the prince's relation to his companions in Eastcheap, than the question of register. When close friends speak to each other, especially friends of the same sex, their language often takes the form of ironic insults: so a man introducing a friend to his fiancée might say 'This is Peter, who's been the bane of my life for ten years', or 'Come and meet this layabout' (or 'this idiot', 'this parasite', or whatever other abusive term he likes to use). Colleagues at work, too, often use insults as a form of banter. It is of course necessary to feel sure that such ironic remarks will not be taken seriously.

This is regularly the way Prince Hal addresses Falstaff. In their very first scene together he responds to Falstaff's question

'What time of day is it?' by telling him that he is so 'fat-witted' that he has 'forgotten to demand that truly which thou wouldst truly know'. This is banter, or – to use a technical term from linguistics – language used for phatic communication, that is, to establish the relationship between the speaker and the person spoken to. Irony is very common in such language use, and anyone who has made a joking remark that has fallen flat or caused offence is aware of the danger of using irony. Hal's remarks do not fall flat or cause offence, since he is the prince and no-one is likely to be rash enough to take offence; but they are subject to the constant possibility, as with all irony, of being taken straight, that is, as an expression of hostility, contempt or dismissal.

It is not only with Falstaff that this is the case. We have looked at the prince's sudden switch of register at the end of his tormenting of Francis; and for a more complex example we can look at the conversation with Poins in Act II, Scene ii of Part 2. The prince begins 'Before God I am exceeding weary', and Poins' reply 'I had thought weariness durst not have attacked one of high blood' leads to an exchange about the prince's rank, and the fact that he is mixing with social inferiors – like Poins:

> What a disgrace is it to me to remember thy name! Or to know thy face tomorrow! Or to take note how many pair of silk stockings thou hast   (II. ii. 12)

– leads to a bawdy remark on Poins' clothing.

Later in the scene comes a pompously joking letter from Falstaff which says nothing of substance, and includes this remark: 'Be not too familiar with Poins, for he misuses thy favour so much that he swears thou art to marry his sister Nell.' No doubt they laugh together about Falstaff's self-importance, and then Hal says 'But do you use me thus, Ned? Must I marry your sister?' Poins replies 'God send the wench no worse fortune. But I never said so.'

All through this scene it is difficult to be certain about the irony. Does the prince really think it 'a disgrace' to mix with Poins and to remember his name, or is he playing the expected role of a prince as part of the joke? The fact that they are discussing the prince's reaction to his father's illness makes the irony even more complex. Poins, asked what he would think if the prince wept, replies 'I would think thee a most princely hypocrite', and the prince agrees that 'it would be every man's thought', adding 'Thou art a blessed fellow, to think as every man thinks.' But the prince has just said that his heart 'bleeds inwardly that my father is sick', and we are surely meant to think that genuine: the loving son and future king is for a moment struggling to emerge from the ironies of Eastcheap.

Hal's language is full of ambiguities: emotions that might be genuine and might not, insults that might be ironic and might be intended. As readers, we can savour these alternatives; but when the play is performed the actors need to decide. Is Hal to laugh, and perhaps slap Poins on the back, when he says 'What a disgrace it is in me to remember thy name', or is he to say it in earnest? And what of Poins' sister? We do not know whether Poins really said this, but the actor needs to know. Is the prince smiling and relaxed when he asks if it's true, or is he offended? Is Poins' reply light-hearted or is he frightened, realising he has gone too far? I have seen the scene played both ways, and both are effective: but we cannot play it both ways at once. Ambiguities that the reader might notice and savour mean, in the theatre, the possibility of playing a scene in different ways.

One other point in the treatment of Hal's youth must strike the reader who compares Shakespeare with the sources: that is the removal of the politics. In the last years of Henry IV's reign there was indeed a good deal of conflict between him and the prince: for about two years the prince was the most powerful member of the king's council, and was able to impose his policy of vigorous hostility to France; there were even suggestions (we do not know how well-founded) of a plot to depose the king in favour of his son. In 1411, however, the king was able to reassert his authority and the prince was dismissed from the council, being replaced by his brother Thomas of Clarence.

None of this appears in Shakespeare's version. The king is worried, and we are entertained, by the irresponsible behaviour of Hal, the madcap prince: but there is no suggestion that he represents a focus of political opposition. When the king is reproaching Hal in Part 1 he includes among his faults 'Thy place in council hast thou rudely lost'. It is hard to be sure if this is a reference to the prince's dismissal from the council in 1411 (if it is, Shakespeare has ante-dated it by 8 years!), but if it is then

Shakespeare has replaced what was a political coup by what sounds like a punishment for misbehaviour. In *The Famous Victories* the prince, impatient to succeed to the throne, actually says that he is eager for his father to die, but Shakespeare removed that. And the relationship between the prince and his brother is actually reversed. The historical Duke of Clarence (second son of Henry IV) was a focus of opposition to the prince, and when the king regained his power in 1411 and dismissed the prince, it was Thomas of Clarence who replaced him. In Shakespeare, however, the king is convinced that Thomas is the prince's favourite:

> He loves thee, and thou dost neglect him, Thomas.
> Thou hast a better place in his affection
> Than all thy brothers; cherish it, my boy,

> (2 HIV: IV. iv. 21)

And he then launches into a pleading piece of advice, urging Thomas to use this bond to modify the prince's dangerous moodiness. If Shakespeare was here drawing on the passage in Stow where the king warns Hal against possible trouble from Thomas, then the reversal (now he is warning Thomas against Hal!) must be part of his plan to make sure that the madcap prince is never seen as politically subversive.

The contrast between the madcap prince and the responsible heir to the throne is of course a contrast not only in diction but also in location: Hal behaves in one way in Eastcheap, in another way in court. This is a natural and effective way of pointing the contrast: if the movement from tavern to court is in some way marked on the stage (easy in the modern theatre, and perhaps possible in simplified form in the Elizabethan), then the contrast in register is underlined by a visual contrast. This means of course that in Eastcheap he is always Hal, at court he is always the Prince of Wales, and the play maintains this contrast – with one small exception.

The play-acting in Act II, Scene iv of Part 1 (which is discussed below) is interrupted by the arrival of the sheriff, in search of the robbers: Falstaff hides 'behind the arras' – no doubt in the inner stage – and the prince has a brief, uneasy interview with the sheriff. Immediately the register changes: they speak in verse, the sheriff addresses him as 'my lord', and the atmosphere is quiet but tense. It is quite obvious to us that the prince is lying – he declares that Falstaff 'is not here' – and it may well be obvious to the sheriff, but he cannot of course say so. The prince keeps the sheriff at bay, and pulls rank: 'And so let me entreat you leave the house' and the sheriff must of course obey:

> I will, my lord. There are two gentlemen
> Have in this robbery lost three hundred marks.

(II. iv. 504)

It sounds as if he submits, but cannot leave without registering the fact that he is uneasy, even resentful: he cannot accuse the prince of lying, but he can at least point out that this is a serious matter.

It is an uncomfortable moment. It cannot easily be cut in production, since the sheriff's arrival is necessary to interrupt the play-acting; and since it then serves as a brief reminder that Hal is, after all, the prince, it seems to underline the awkwardness of the gap between his two selves. Once the sheriff has been got rid of, Hal returns to prose, and to the teasing of Falstaff, but also announces that 'the money shall be paid back again, with advantage' – a detail which appeared in Stow, and which has to be mentioned somewhere.

It is hard to know if this short scene is a sign of awkwardness on Shakespeare's part, or a deliberate reminder of the awkwardness of the prince's double life. It is the only moment when the two worlds encounter each other so explicitly.

FALSTAFF

In discussing the Eastcheap scenes we have, inevitably, already begun to discuss Falstaff, the most memorable and popular character in the play. Now we need to look more closely at him.

He was not always called Falstaff. When Shakespeare first wrote the play, the fat knight was called Oldcastle: the name of a real person, as we saw earlier. Since Oldcastle had been a Lollard martyr, and since there is nothing pious or puritanical about Falstaff, the name would certainly have seemed inappropriate to anyone who knew about the real Oldcastle. Whether or not for that reason, Sir Henry Brook, seventh Lord Cobham, who was

29

descended from the second wife of Oldcastle, appears to have objected to what he saw as a slur on the family. For a few months in 1596–7 (just about the time Shakespeare was writing *Henry IV*) Brooke was Lord Chamberlain, and was therefore responsible (through his underling the Master of the Revels) for the control and censorship of the theatres; and he evidently succeeded in making Shakespeare change the name of his character (Sir John Falstaff was also a real person (usually spelt Fastolf), contemporary with Oldcastle, but he evidently had no descendants who objected).

There are a few traces in the text as we have it of the change of name. In the first Eastcheap scene Hal calls Falstaff 'my old lad of the castle'; in one speech heading in Part 2 Falstaff is called 'Old'; and the Epilogue to Part 2 remarks that 'Oldcastle died martyr, and this is not the man', which might well be an apology to the Brook family, as well as an admission that Oldcastle, as a Puritan martyr, had been maligned. There is some evidence that the public continued to remember that he had been called Oldcastle, and that people with Puritan leanings resented the slur. But the change of name was made, and everyone now knows him as Falstaff.

Let us begin with a simple, even naive question: what is Falstaff like? Three points surely belong in the answer: that he is a coward, that he is greedy, and that he is witty. First, cowardice.

The opposite of cowardice is, obviously, courage; and the figure who most clearly represents courage in this play is Hotspur. Falstaff and Hotspur represent two extreme attitudes to fighting, the one avoiding it, the other seeking it out. Since this play shows us an England where there is almost continual fighting, this contrast draws attention to what is central to their characters, and the word used to denote it is 'honour'. Here is Hotspur, whom Douglas describes as 'the king of honour':

> By heaven, methinks it were an easy leap
> To pluck bright honour from the pale-faced moon,
> Or dive into the bottom of the deep,
> Where fathom line could never touch the ground,
> And pluck up drownèd honour by the locks

> (1HIV: I. iii. 199)

'Where fathom line could never touch the ground'. We do not

think of Hotspur as a poetical character (on another occasion he declares his contempt for 'mincing poetry') but when seized with enthusiasm for honour he is so carried away that he lingers on the poetical figure: 'the bottom of the deep' has caught his fancy because it is an image for his beloved honour, and so he allows himself to elaborate on it.

Hotspur's single-minded pursuit of honour aligns him with characters who occur throughout Shakespeare's plays, those who value their own dignity more than anything, who lose their temper easily and are often spoiling for a fight: Tybalt, Laertes, Coriolanus. They never pretend to be any different, and they often divide the sympathies of audiences: some admire their refusal to compromise, others see them as aggressive and pig-headed; and they all die fighting. Hotspur is probably the most attractive of them, but he too reveals to us that the ideal of honour is noble but narrow.

Falstaff, too, talks about honour – most famously in his soliloquy just before the battle towards the end of Part 1 (V. i. 27). Not only is this speech in prose, but it is prose that reaches the extreme of matter-of-factness: 'Can honour set to a leg? No. Or take away the grief of a wound? No. So what is honour? A word.' If we now think back to Hotspur's speech, we can see that we are being told that Hotspur had mistaken words for something real, that Hotspur, the practical man of action, had allowed himself to be deceived by words and their magic. Falstaff, however, looking round the battlefield, sees reality: Sir Walter Blunt is lying there dead, and he observes: 'I like not such grinning honour as Sir Walter hath.' *Grinning* is a brilliant touch: the dead Sir Walter can no longer smile at anything, so that 'grinning' is an image for the hideousness of death; but at the same time we can imagine him mocking the uselessness of abstractions like honour.

Cowardice, we can see, drifts into cynicism. We can say that cynicism is a rationalisation of cowardice, an attempt to pass off as objective reflection what is really just personal fear; or we can say that cowardice is a perfectly rational way to behave if you are cynical about the values which courage defends. Admirers of Hotspur will say the first, admirers of Falstaff the second.

Next is Falstaff's greed. This could be said to be his most prominent characteristic, since he no doubt owes his size to his greed, though the Falstaff we see is greedy for drink and money rather than food – indeed, the most famous sentence about his greed, spoken by the prince as he reads the tavern bill of the snoring Falstaff ('O monstrous! But one ha'pennyworth of bread to this intolerable deal of sack!') actually contrasts Falstaff's drinking with eating. In Part 2, what we are mainly shown is greed for money: Falstaff quite shamelessly uses his recruiting as a way to profit from bribes, and uses Justice Shallow as someone to borrow money from (which probably, even if he had not been repudiated by the king, he had no intention of paying back).

And here too cynicism lurks behind what we see. Falstaff's method of raising soldiers is probably the most corrupt thing about him. He describes his practice in Part 1: 'I press me none but good householders, yeomen's sons, enquire me out contracted bachelors' – that is, those who will be eager to bribe their way out of the army; and the result of this is that Falstaff has pocketed 'three hundred and odd pounds' (a huge sum, of course, in the fifteenth century), and ends up with 'a hundred and fifty tattered prodigals lately come from swine-keeping, from eating draff and husks' (IV. ii. 11–46); and in Part 2 (III. ii) we see his recruiting in action as he presses the comically named Mouldy, Shadow, Wart and Feeble, ignores Shallow's advice, and ends up with those who don't bribe him. This is not the sentimentalist's Falstaff, the cheerful good companion, but an unscrupulously corrupt official cashing in on his official position. The prince, when he sees Falstaff's soldiers, remarks on what 'pitiful rascals' they are, and Falstaff's reply is one of the most powerful lines in the play:

> Tut, tut, good enough to toss, food for powder, food for powder, they'll fill a pit as well as better. Tush man, mortal men, mortal men. (IV. ii. 63)

This is one of those moments when Shakespeare seems to take us into the world of Brecht, the most cynical, down-to-earth and brilliant of modern dramatists. The tone, as the interjections make clear ('Tut, tut' . . . 'Tush man') is casual and untroubled; taken as a reply to the accusation of corruption it is totally cynical. But of course it also a comment on the total irrelevance of moral considerations when blood is the argument. It is the bitter underside of Hotspur's glorification of honour, a reminder of what civil war really means. It is too truthful for laughter.

And then wit. Falstaff is himself quite conscious of this, and amuses himself by saying 'I am not only witty in myself, but the cause of wit in other men', taking credit for the jokes made at his expense. We are never shown Falstaff drunk, as we are shown Silence, for a drunken character may be the cause of wit in other men, but would not himself be witty, and Falstaff, though jokes are made at his expense (especially by Hal) is not a mere butt. His detailed account of how sack is good for one's wits ('it ascends me into the brain . . . makes it apprehensive, quick, forgetive,' (that is, like a forge) 'full of nimble, fiery and delectable shapes') says nothing about the ability of alcohol to deprive us of control, and so joins together Falstaff's greed and his wit..

Falstaff is always quoting scripture – more often, perhaps, than any other character in Shakespeare. In his very first conversation with Hal (1HIV: I. ii, 78ff) he breaks suddenly into what the audience would have recognised as Puritan language – and some of them, no doubt, would have smiled at as Puritan cant: 'But Hal, I prithee trouble me no more with vanity . . . Before I knew thee, Hal, I knew nothing; and now am I, if a man should speak truly, little better than one of the wicked.' The joke here of course is that Hal could more appropriately have said this to Falstaff; and Hal pricks the bubble of this mock-pious talk by suggesting a robbery tomorrow, which Falstaff eagerly accepts; then

> HAL. I see a good amendment of life in thee – from praying to purse-taking.
> FAL. Why Hal, 'tis my vocation, Hal. 'Tis no sin for a man to labour in his vocation.

> (I. ii. 102)

Falstaff is citing 1 Corinthians 7:20, which in the Geneva Bible (the one most used in the 1590s) runs 'let every man abide in the same vocation wherein he was called'; it was a favourite text of Puritan divines. In the next act, after Falstaff has been caught out in his lies, he tells the hostess to close the doors, adding 'Watch tonight, pray tomorrow.' Here he is citing (and twisting)

Matthew 26:41 'Watch and pray, that ye enter not into temptation' – with wordplay on 'pray' and 'prey'. And so on, whenever he appears. There may be no character in Shakespeare who uses Scripture more often.

It would obviously be naive to claim that this indicates that he still has attributes of the devout Lollard Sir John Oldcastle, though it is just possible that Oldcastle's piety suggested this trait to Shakespeare. It would be equally naive to start constructing a biography of Falstaff that included a pious childhood with biblical instruction. His habit of citing Scripture is functional: it adds a dimension to Falstaff as we see him, showing us that he is made of parody, and especially parody of Scripture. It is a reminder that, as Antonio said of Shylock in *The Merchant of Venice*, 'the devil can cite scripture for his purpose.'

In the theatrical tradition that lay behind Shakespeare – the religious drama of the Middle Ages that was still being performed when he was a young man – the wittiest character was the Vice, the personage who was both devil and clown, who addressed the audience direct, made jokes, took them into his confidence, and indulged in constant wordplay, so that a connection is assumed between theatrical self-consciousness (talking direct to the audience, taking them into one's confidence) and wit. Not only does Falstaff derive from this tradition, he is actually referred to by the prince as 'thou reverent Vice, thou grave Iniquity ('Iniquity' was sometimes the name of the clown/devil figure) – a reminder to the audience of the theatrical tradition, and perhaps of the function of Falstaff in the play.

TWO DEATHS AND A RESURRECTION

Falstaff is full of surprises, and the Falstaff plot full of echoes and parodies of the main plot. The most extreme of these occurs at the end of Part 1, and it is impossible to decide just how subversive of the main plot it really is.

That Falstaff should pretend to be dead in order to save his life is not surprising, and he uses the trick in order to survive his unexpected encounter with Douglas; what is surprising, however, is that this comic moment should take place during the fight between Hal and Hotspur. In modern productions these two often go offstage for a while (not difficult to manage during a sword fight), then after Falstaff has escaped from Douglas they return for the climax and the death of Hotspur. This leaves the prince alone with two bodies: Hotspur, over whom he delivers a conventional and dignified speech

> This earth that bears thee dead
> Bears not alive so stout a gentleman

> (v. iv. 91)

– and Falstaff, whom he only then notices:

> Poor Jack, farewell!
> I could have better spared a better man.

> (v. iv. 102)

The shift in register is immediately striking: 'brave Percy' gives place to the familiar 'poor Jack', and conventional tribute to puns: 'death hath not struck so fat a deer today, | Though many dearer.' Only in the last couplet, when he turns again to Percy, does the prince's speech regain some of its dignity:

> Embowelled will I see thee by and by,
> Till then in blood by noble Percy lie.

> (v. iv. 108)

But this comparatively solemn moment is immediately parodied, as Falstaff sits up with an echo that never fails to get a laugh in the theatre: 'Embowelled?'

The sub-plot of an Elizabethan play, as is often remarked, can parallel and parody the main plot: but never is there a more violent juxtaposition, and a more subversive parody, than this. The single combat which forms the heroic climax is immediately turned into farce, as violent death is juxtaposed with its gross parody. Then, as if that was not subversive enough, Falstaff parodies the killing of Hotspur by giving him 'a new wound in your thigh', and parodies the prince's triumph by announcing that he'll claim to have killed Hotspur himself – which the prince, with a shrug, allows him to get away with.

For a few moments, we have been taken from the heroic story to the world of folk drama, of the Mummers' Play in which St George fights the Turkish knight, and one or the other is killed and brought back to life. Some regard this folk play as an echo or parody of the resurrection of Christ, and it certainly is an irreverent treatment of potentially sacred material. In *Henry IV* the serious story is followed so promptly by its parody that we cannot fail to ask how radically it is being undermined. Is the heroic plot strong enough to withstand being mocked, or are we left with an aftertaste that will linger and permeate our whole conception of the play. In the theatre, the director may nudge us one way or the other, but the answer must be ours.

FALSTAFF 'S WORLD

'Company, villainous company, hath undone me,' complains Falstaff jokingly – and whether they have undone him or he them is anyone's guess. The company in which Falstaff mixes is a gigantic parody of the official moral values, and like most parodies it leaves us uncertain whether it is a contrast or an exposure.

The parody – the world of the sub-plot – is as prominent as the main plot: in Part 1 it occupies almost as much space, in Part 2 slightly more. The inhabitants of this world are made out of what the Elizabethans called humours (stock figures dominated by one emotion or character trait), but touched by Shakespeare's genius they are vivid and memorable in a way that the humour-figures of the Elizabethan stage seldom are. Pistol, for instance, who is introduced into Part 2, no doubt to give more variety to the Eastcheap scenes, is a version of the braggart who is a coward beneath his boasting: the hostess describes him as a 'swaggerer', and everything he says is quarrelsome bluster. Of course Falstaff too is a variant of the boastful coward, and one of the functions of Pistol is to show how much variety is possible in different versions of the same humour. As a character, Pistol is simple enough; but the simplicity of the character drawing contrasts strongly with the rich variety of his verbal resources. Much of what he says is in verse, often larded with quotations – and misquotations – from the heroic plays of an earlier generation, often those of the rival theatre company. He is almost incapable of saying anything without 'swaggering' – the hostess's term, which describes his language as much as his behaviour. Pistol is absurd, but at the same time embodies a delight in extravagant language which has a kind of zany charm. Bardolph is a much simpler figure, the butt of repetitive jokes about his red nose; and, for a reason that is not clear, he is given the same name as Lord Bardolph, a character from the main plot who appears among the rebels in Part 2.

The hostess of the tavern is also a stock figure, In Part 1 she is known simply as 'Hostess' (though she is named once) and she has a husband (though he does not appear); in Part 2 she is a widow, and is more often given her name (Mistress Quickly). This is not necessarily inconsistent, but Shakespeare does seem to have grown more interested in her in Part 2, without troubling too much about consistency with the character who had already appeared in the first Part. In Act II, Scene i, where she is trying to get Falstaff arrested for debt, she is given a wonderfully rambling speech describing the occasion on which, she claims, he proposed to her, 'sitting in my Dolphin chamber, at the round table, by a sea-coal fire, upon Wednesday in Wheeson'. The prose of common folk, anchored in the concrete, has a vividness and particularity that the dignity of the verse can seldom attain to. But her wish to marry Falstaff and become a lady does not prevent her from procuring the prostitute Doll Tearsheet for him: it's almost as if marriage and sex have no connection with each other. Mistress Quickly wishes to marry Falstaff because it represents social rise and respectability, and has little to do with sex, or with procreation: no one in Eastcheap seems to have children. Two female characters are therefore necessary: the hostess, whether married or widowed, is too respectable to sit on Falstaff's knee, caressing him; Doll, in contrast, reminds one of the pleasures and corruptions of flesh, and is both more disgusting and more moving, sitting on Falstaff's knee and declaring that she loves this old man 'better than I love e'er a scurvy young boy of them all': both a tearful compliment to Falstaff and a bitter reflection on her life as a prostitute. This brief episode casts a sudden light on Falstaff too, who responds to Doll's affection with a rueful awareness of mortality: 'Peace, good Doll, do not speak like a death's head; do not bid me remember mine end.' The literary pun on 'die', with its sexual meaning, seems to lie behind the sudden sad realism of this remark, made at the moment when the prince and Poins appear, disguised as drawers; so that Poins' contemptuous 'Shall we beat him before his whore?' can sound like a sudden crude coarseness, a vulgarisation of a complex scene. To ask whether Doll is 'sincere' in what she says is to ask for an oversimplified reading of this mixture of pathos and absurdity, satire and sexual desire. For this effect it is not necessary for Doll to be a complex or individualised character: she comes to life when – only when – she receives the author's full attention.

In *Henry V* Shakespeare seems to have grown careless again: by now the hostess has married Pistol (her earlier dislike of him quietly forgotten!) and we learn – for the first time – that her first name is Nell – though earlier in Part 2, Falstaff refers to 'old mistress Ursula, whom I have weekly sworn to marry' – and whether this is Mistress Quickly or another woman not elsewhere mentioned we cannot say and Shakespeare, perhaps, did not care. When Pistol, in France, receives news of her death, he calls her Doll – not, surely, Pistol's mistake, but Shakespeare's. Pistol (and those of his companions who haven't been hanged) now has to return to the disreputable underworld of London – a world full of criminal ex-soldiers like him, and of Nells and Dolls and Ursulas indistinguishable from one another.

Doll and Mistress Quickly also appear briefly in Act V, Scene iv, where they are being dragged off by the beadles to be whipped: a rather nasty scene for modern tastes, which nowadays is often dropped in performance. It has one clear point: it must be part of the clean-up that the reformed prince is now going to see carried out, and so prepares us for the rejection scene that is already looming. And it does give us a glimpse that we get nowhere else of the London underworld. Doll claims that she is pregnant, which would make the whole episode much nastier, but the beadle does not believe her, and maintains that she has stuffed a cushion into her clothes (line 15): it is left to us to decide who to believe. A production could no doubt show her stuffing the cushion in, but that would be the director's decision, with no textual warrant – though it is tempting to add that it would have been particularly effective on the Elizabethan stage, where it would be a coarse reminder, a kind of wink to the audience, that the part was being played by a boy. And though the whipping of prostitutes was by no means unknown in Elizabethan England, a more serious note is introduced by the beadle saying 'there hath been a man or two lately killed about her': life in Eastcheap does not consist only of playing holidays.

A word about the language of Eastcheap. It is soon obvious to the modern reader of Shakespeare that his prose has dated much more than his verse, and the language of the common folk more than the language of the nobles. The characters of the sub-plot speak an English that is racier, more colloquial, and contains far more slang, more puns, and more verbal evasions than that of the aristocrats – and for this reason, it is much harder for us to follow. The conversation between the carriers (delivery men), Gadshill and the chamberlain, in Act II, Scene i of Part 1, grows almost incomprehensible at times, most of all when the carriers are speaking among themselves (Gadshill may be of a slightly higher social standing than the others, so that the conversation is closer to standard English when he is present). But when the first carrier asks the ostler 'I prithee, Tom, beat Cut's saddle, put a few flocks in the point; poor jade is wrung in the withers out of all cess', it is only with the help of the Oxford dictionary – or an editor – that we can translate it into 'Please, Tom, soften the horse's saddle by beating it, and put a few tufts of wool in the pommel. The poor nag is chafed excessively ('out of all cess') between the shoulder-blades.'

That is bad enough; but when the subject is the human body things get even harder. Slang tends to be at its most volatile – and so most obscure – when dealing with the body, and especially with sex, so that a speech like this of Falstaff's to Doll Tearsheet leaves us with a general sense of its indecency but not understanding much:

> Your brooches, pearls and ouches – for to serve bravely is to come halting off, you know; to come off the breach, with his pike bent bravely; and to surgery bravely; to venture upon the charged chambers bravely...
>
> (2HIV: II. iv. 48)

Editors have suggested that the first five words, and perhaps part of the rest, is a quotation from some song or ballad, but if so it has not been identified. *Ouch* is a brooch, and can also mean a carbuncle or pimple. The passage is full of military terms, all of which can carry a sexual meaning (as military terms so often can!), including a reference to venereal disease.

Exploring the history of colloquial speech, and its possibilities of sexual and other innuendo, can be fascinating, and one of the richest sources for the history of popular culture. And the reader of Shakespeare who has the leisure – and the resources – to explore prose like this can learn a great deal; but it clearly poses a problem in the modern theatre. A good actor who understands such a speech can no doubt convey its flavour to a responsive audience, but the experience of getting the gist without really understanding, like that of hearing a play in a foreign language we do not understand, is obviously limited. The actor and director are therefore likely to have to choose between using a modernised text or cutting the speech.

And finally, to Gloucestershire. On his way to Galtree Falstaff stops at the estate of his old friend Shallow, now a local landowner and magistrate, in order to recruit the 'company of foot' that the prince had procured for him in Part 1. Some scholars have questioned whether Gloucester lay on the route from London to Galtree, and there are one or two clues (like the mention of 'Stamford fair') suggesting that Shallow was originally located in Lincolnshire. But of course the geography does not matter: this is rural England, a glimpse of the land the politicians are fighting about, and we might as well call it Gloucestershire.

These scenes show Shakespearean comedy at its most brilliantly entertaining. Justice Shallow, as a humour figure, is of course named for his most notable quality, which is stupidity, and the predictable shallowness of much of what he says. So when Falstaff makes his (sometimes rather laboured) jokes about the names of his recruits – saying of Mouldy, for instance, 'tis the more time thou wert used', Shallow finds it necessary to explain the joke, very repetitively, to anyone who will listen, and his plodding explanation is much more entertaining than the joke itself. Similarly, when Bardolph remarks, rather pompously, that Falstaff is unmarried because 'a soldier is better accommodated than with a wife', Shallow is so impressed by Bardolph's vocabulary that he can't stop explaining the meaning. Shallow's greeting to his 'cousin Silence' – two old men reminiscing about the past – is both comic and pathetic: not alternately, but the most comic moments are often the most pathetic. Shallow moves between matter-of-fact questions about the present ('How a good yoke of bullocks at Stamford fair?') and trite, repetitive reflections on mortality ('Death, as the Psalmist saith, is certain to all). If we remember that this takes place during the king's mortal illness, we can see the close relationship between the two plots, how the comedy of the sub-plot can parody but also express the sadness of the main plot. Falstaff finds Shallow ridiculous, but he too is part of the pathos: a tiny verbal detail, brilliant but so unobtrusive we might not notice it, makes this clear. When he is left alone, Falstaff tells the audience how easily he sees through Shallow. 'Lord, Lord,' he remarks, 'how subject we old men are to this vice of lying!' (III. ii, 296). He is talking about Shallow, but he says '*we* old men', including himself almost without noticing, so that he is not only the commentator but the subject of the remark: and we have heard plenty of Falstaff's lies already. But he is not repenting of them, he just includes himself with a shrug. It is a very similar effect to his shrug to the prince: 'food for powder, food for powder.' As if to say, what else can you expect?

It is not only lies but also corruption that we find in Gloucestershire, for that too is not limited to politicians. Falstaff, observing that Shallow has 'land and beefs', decides to return to Gloucestershire on his way back to London in order to fleece him (which he does); and Shallow's motives in dispensing hospitality are just as selfish: 'I will use him well,' he remarks to his servant Davy, 'a friend i'th'court is better than a penny in purse.' Corruption is endemic in rural England as it is in politics: indeed, corruption is part of its charm. Shallow is a magistrate, and Davy asks him to 'countenance', that is, to support his friend Visor against a complainant; Shallow replies 'there is many complaints, Davy, against that Visor.' Davy's reply is a glorious mixture of shrewdness and absurdity: 'An honest man, sir, is able to speak for himself, when a knave is not. I have served your worship truly, sir, this eight years; and if I cannot once or twice in a quarter bear out a knave against an honest man, I have but very little credit with your worship.' It is quite common in Shakespeare for the truest remarks to come from the stupidest people, and Davy has unwittingly shown us the whole basis of loyalty and faction that underlies the main

41

plot. Gloucestershire is more fun than the court, but morally no different.

THE LORD CHIEF JUSTICE

An amusing pastime – and perhaps more than a pastime – for critics of Shakespeare is to think about the scenes he did not write – and ask why. Why did he not write the recognition scene between Leontes and his daughter at the end of *The Winter's Tale*, giving us merely a description of what happened by a courtier? We cannot answer such questions, merely consider possible explanations. In this case, the question is: Why are we not shown either Prince Hal striking the Chief Justice, or the prince being taken to prison? The episode was well known, and it occurs in *The Famous Victories*, but in Shakespeare it is only mentioned. In fact the first encounter we are shown between Hal and the Chief Justice takes place only after he has become king. Act V, Scene ii opens with a scene at court, the Chief Justice and the princes waiting for the new king to arrive, and the Justice is clearly nervous, believing he has done no wrong but knowing that the young king loves him not. When the two of them meet, the king begins in apparent anger:

> What! Rate, rebuke, and roughly send to prison
> Th'immediate heir of England?

(2HIV: v. ii. 70)

After a vigorous defence from the Chief Justice of his actions, the king declares him to have been right, and says 'You shall be as a father to my youth' – and indeed uses him to reproach Falstaff in the final scene. It is not clear whether the king was resentful and then was brought round by the Chief Justice's defence of himself, or had always intended to adopt him as a counsellor and was just teasing in his opening remarks.

We have seen the Chief Justice earlier in the play – encountering not the prince, but Falstaff, reproaching him for his way of life in Act I, Scene ii, and intervening in the hostess's attempt to arrest Falstaff for debt (I.ii), but this is the first time he encounters Hal. The Justice is clearly a counterweight to Falstaff: both are father figures to the prince, one representing

42

responsibility, the other misrule; but the Justice is also curiously external to the action. All his scenes except the last look like chance encounters, conversations when he happens to meet people in the street; perhaps we should link this with the fact that – unusually for so prominent a character – he is never named. It's almost as if his symbolic role in the play prevents him from taking on too definite an identity of his own.

THE REJECTION OF FALSTAFF

As we have seen, the very first of the Eastcheap scenes ends with the prince's soliloquy informing us that he is going to emerge from his low-life companions like the sun emerging from 'the base contagious clouds'. We therefore know from near the beginning – and most of the Elizabethan audience probably knew in advance – that Falstaff is going to be rejected. What we do not know in advance, however, is that he is to be rejected twice.

The second and final rejection occurs where we would expect it – at the end of Part 2, and it makes a powerful and no doubt expected climax. Falstaff is visiting Justice Shallow when he learns that the old king is dead and his moment has come. That moment has of course been anticipated all through both plays, as in the conversation between Hal and Falstaff in their very first encounter, when Falstaff says 'Do not thou, when thou art king, hang a thief (Act I, Scene ii, 60), and Hal replies 'No, thou shalt': this can mean 'No, thou shalt hang thieves' (that is, be the hangman), and also, if we strain the meaning a little, taking 'hang' as intransitive, 'thou shalt hang as a thief'. So when Pistol arrives in Gloucestershire with the news that Hal really is king, we have a scene (Act V, Scene iii) that is breathless with excitement: Pistol, of course, has to do a spot of swaggering before coming to the point, and makes a meal of the announcement ('Under which king, Besonian? Speak or die!'); when the news finally comes out, Falstaff rushes about calling for his boots, announcing that he will ride all night, and making promises to everyone: 'Master Robert Shallow, choose thou what office thou wilt in the land,'tis thine.' The most resonant of his excited remarks is surely his concluding sentence: 'Blessed are they that have been my friends, and woe to my Lord Chief Justice.' The lingering open vowel of 'woe' can allow Falstaff's delight to echo through the theatre, while also giving us a frightening glimpse of what is apparently going to happen to England.

What actually happens, of course, is that Prince Hal, now Henry V, refuses to know him. His eager greeting during the coronation procession ('God save thee, my sweet boy!') receives, as response, a very formal and unequivocal rejection: 'I know thee not, old man. Fall to thy prayers!' Some critics, and no doubt many more audiences, have complained that such a public and solemn rejection is particularly cruel; no doubt it could be defended by pointing out that this was Falstaff's fault, since he it was who chose to make the confrontation a public one. But this would be to treat dramatic necessities as if they were real-life occurrences. The rejection of Falstaff has to be formal and unequivocal – and therefore public – not just because Falstaff made it public, but because it is the climax of the play.

Theatrically, the rejection of Falstaff is extreme: everything in the scene is designed to point the contrast between him and Hal – or rather, as we must now say, between him and the king. Hal is for the first time dressed as befits royalty; he is part of – indeed, the climax of – the coronation procession. Falstaff, since he has ridden all night, might well appear even scruffier than usual. The king is centre stage and protected from the crowd; Falstaff is a gatecrasher. When they speak, the contrast in register is extreme, between Falstaff's prose and the king's verse, Falstaff's familiarity ('my sweet boy') and the king's refusal, at first, to address him direct ('My Lord Chief Justice, speak to that vain man').

We can even, if the actor is able to bring this out, *hear* the change in register. A few lines into his speech of rejection, the king says

> Leave gormandising; know the grave doth gape
> For thee thrice wider than for other men.

(v. v. 56)

No doubt these two lines will be delivered in the same stern tone as the rest of the speech: yet they play upon Falstaff's size

44

to suggest the kind of joke Hal was always making at his expense, indeed that Falstaff himself might have made. And Falstaff presumably hears this, and was about to respond to the joke, when he is cut off: 'Reply not to me with a fool-born jest.' It's as if the king is saying – to underline the unfairness – that he is allowed to make one of the old jokes, but it is no longer a joke, it is now a piece of moralising, so Falstaff is not allowed to join in. And he is saying to the audience that the joking is over, that if they think he was saying something funny, they were mistaken.

'I know thee not, old man': once those words are spoken, the play is virtually over. Nothing remains except tidying up: a glimpse of Falstaff's reaction ('I shall be sent for in private to him' – a desperate attempt to avoid facing what has happened) and a short conversation between Prince John of Lancaster and the Lord Chief Justice that makes it clear that the new king is going to take his father's Machiavellian advice ('busy giddy minds | With foreign quarrels'), thus preparing us for the next play, *Henry V*. The real ending was the new king's speech of rejection, and it had to sound like an ending: dignified, uninterrupted, and in the expected register of royalty.

That is the climax and conclusion: but we have already had a rejection of Falstaff. In Act II, Scene iv of Part 1, Hal and Falstaff have been discussing what the prince is going to say to his father when he meets him, and they decide to act their own impromptu play about it, first with Falstaff and then with Hal pretending to be the king. A play within the play is common enough in Elizabethan drama, but this one is no mere interlude or entertainment, since the parts are tightly bound to the main action: Falstaff and Hal are playing themselves, or each other, on something which is no laughing matter. No wonder the hostess is made to remark 'O Jesu, this is excellent sport, i'faith.' We need to be reminded that it is sport, because it is also so serious.

Falstaff, playing the king, puts in a word for himself: 'there is a virtuous man whom I have often noted in thy company.' Part of the fun, but there is no harm in a little nudge on his own behalf. Then, when they change places, and Hal plays the king, the exchange, to begin with, is also part of the game, but at the same time he is playing what he is going to become, and he delivers a mock denunciation of Falstaff that is all too real: 'a devil that haunts thee in the likeness of an old fat man'. It is in

45

this speech that we get our reminder of dramatic tradition ('that reverent Vice, that grey Iniquity, that Father Ruffian, that Vanity in years'). And then, after Falstaff has shrugged off the possibility of rejection with a piece of bluster ('Banish plump Jack, and banish all the world'), the prince, now the king, is terrifyingly blunt in his response: 'I do. I will.' Most actors deliver this remark in all seriousness, and there is no return to fun and games. It has the same effect as Hal's opening soliloquy, but raises no awkward questions about whether the speaker is stepping out of character to become a chorus. Hal has stepped out of character in a perfectly obvious way, by acting a play. It is the most brilliant scene in *Henry IV*, deeply embedded in the conventions of the stage.

Why is Falstaff rejected twice? In a sense the question is unnecessary: each scene is so brilliant that we wouldn't wish to lose either of them; but we can still ask what we learn about the play, and about drama in general, by getting them both. It is clear, isn't it, that there is an extra dimension to the mock rejection in Part 1: this is drama as metadrama, the acting of a scene plus an awareness that what we are seeing is *acting*, so that we remain within the world of Eastcheap while being taken out of it. If it was just a Feast of Fools we would know that it is not to be taken seriously; this is both a Feast of Fools, and also serious. Then when the real rejection comes, it is merely serious. It is now like a coronation speech, which spectators are not allowed to interrupt or make fun of. The rich complexity of drama has now been switched off: Henry is king in earnest. It is necessary for the play to end in this way, so that it can offer us a piece of ritual, as a reminder that becoming king is a serious matter; but in dramatic terms this reminder is also an impoverishment. So we were first given a rejection that was part of the play, to set against a rejection that tells us that playing is over.

PART 1: PART 2

It was not unusual in Shakespeare's time, as it is not unknown today, to write two or more plays that form a series: Marlowe's *Tamburlaine*, possibly the most successful play performed in the first years of Shakespeare's career, is two full-length plays, and the prologue to Part 2 tells us that it was the success of the first play that 'made our poet pen his second part'; *Bussy d'Ambois*, George Chapman's most successful play, was followed a few years later by *The Revenge of Bussy*: since Bussy is killed at the end of the first play, the only way Chapman could write a sequel was to make his brother the hero, and to bring Bussy's ghost into the action. These are clearly examples of the sequel being an afterthought. Nothing is known about the planning of Shakespeare's earlier trilogy about Henry VI, or even whether it is accurate to call it a trilogy rather than three separate plays.

There has been a great deal of discussion and speculation about the two parts of *Henry IV*: were they planned as a unity, or was the first part meant to be complete and the sequel added because of its success? Nobody knows, and scholars are divided: the most popular theory is probably that Shakespeare decided, in the course of writing the first part, that it needed to be two plays – either because he had too much material, or because he had a success on his hands. We cannot know, but it does seem clear that Part 1 ends with a virtual admission that matters are unfinished:

> Rebellion in this land shall lose his sway,
> Meeting the check of such another day,
> And since this business so fair is done,
> Let us not leave till all our own be won.

> (v. v. 41)

These concluding lines are in the future tense: rebellion has not lost his sway yet, but will lose it if the king has another such victory (this military use of 'day' is not uncommon). If this is a promise of a sequel, it could reveal that when he wrote these lines Shakespeare intended to end the second play with a battle as well, in which case he thought better of it later. As for the second couplet, though it is spoken by the king, it is not difficult to imagine it being spoken by the actor playing the king, in which case it would be a kind of brief epilogue. 'Since this business so fair is done' would then mean 'since the play has been so successful', and the last line would be announcing that the company are not going to leave the subject till they have exhausted it, and won the applause of the audience.

One thing that we do know, however, is that when an

Elizabethan play has a sequel the two were not often performed in succession: the evidence we have about performance schedules shows no tendency to offer the two parts on successive days. If the two were to be thought of as a unity, this would depend on the interest and memory of members of the audience. This contrasts markedly with modern practice: it is probably more common than not nowadays for a company which performs one of the plays to perform the other as well, perhaps even to offer the whole tetralogy. Modern audiences, as a result, are more likely than Elizabethan audiences to experience the unity of the series.

We cannot, then, profitably discuss the unity – or lack of unity – of the two parts in terms of Shakespeare's intentions; what we can do, however, is look at the result, and think about the problems posed by the fact of two plays, and the way these problems have been solved – if they have. The main problem will clearly be repetition: does the same effect have to occur twice? The episode in which this is most prominent is the reconciliation between father and son. If we are to be shown Prince Hal's wild youth and then shown its redemption, there has to be a reconciliation in each play. So in Part 1 there is a long scene (III. ii) depicting the 'private conference' between father and son, in which the king delivers a long and detailed rebuke at the 'inordinate and low desires', the 'barren pleasures, rude society' of his son, and makes a comparison between the way Percy outshines Hal and the way he himself had earlier outshone Richard: 'And even as I was then is Percy now.' We are clearly being invited to think about what happened in *Richard II*, which the Elizabethan audience could only do by remembering, but today we can of course look at the text and make the comparison. When we do this, it is not easy to be sure how well they fit. The king now insists that his popularity in contrast to Richard was due to his being 'seldom seen':

> Had I so lavish of my presence been,
> So common-hackneyed in the eyes of men,
> So rude and cheap to vulgar company,

(III .ii. 39)

then 'opinion', which helped him to the crown, would not have done so. Hal, in contrast, has been making himself 'common-hackneyed'. Now in *Richard II* there is an account, by Richard himself, of Bolingbroke's 'courtship to the common people' before he went into exile:

> How he did seem to dive into their hearts
> With humble and familiar courtesy;
> What reverence he did throw away on slaves,
> Wooing poor craftsmen with the craft of smiles.

(Richard II: I. iv. 25)

This sounds very different from Bolingbroke's later account of himself. Richard's disdainful description ('Off goes his bonnet to an oyster wench') does not suggest the careful reserve that Henry IV now claims he showed. We can of course claim that Bolingbroke has forgotten his own earlier behaviour, or that he is making it up in order to exaggerate the contrast with his son; or we can claim that Shakespeare has forgotten it.

Hal does not – indeed cannot – say much while the reproach is being delivered; when it is finished, he declares, at some length, that he 'will redeem all this on Percy's head'. What else can he say? Since the play is moving towards its climax in the encounter between him and Hotspur, he cannot actually redeem himself until that happens, and if we listen carefully to Hal's defence we can hardly fail to notice that it is all in the future tense: 'the time will come', 'I will call him to so strict account', 'I will tear the reckoning from his heart'. The king, however, does not listen so sceptically, and responds by saying 'A hundred thousand rebels die in this' – a line which I have never heard an actor deliver cynically.

We are not even two-thirds of the way through the play when this reconciliation between Hal and his father takes place; the climax of his redemption – the fight with Hotspur – is still about half-an-hour away. Of course there is plenty of action to fill this space, but it is necessary to ensure that the audience remains aware that we now have a new version of the prince. Two speeches serve this purpose, and both of them are given to Sir Richard Vernon, one of the rebels. In Act IV, Scene i Hotspur, preparing for battle, makes a disparaging reference to 'the nimble-footed madcap Prince of Wales', and Vernon responds with what is perhaps the most lyrically enthusiastic piece of descriptive writing in the play, comparing him to 'feathered Mercury ', and telling how he

> Vaulted with such ease into his seat
> As if an angel dropped down from the clouds.

> (IV. i. 107–8)

Four scenes later there is a similar exchange. Hotspur is informed that the prince has challenged him to single combat. He is less contemptuous this time, and obviously wishes to take up the challenge. He asks how the prince showed, and once again Vernon delivers a speech of glowing praise, telling us that 'England did never owe so sweet a hope'. Hotspur's response is dignified and respectful, and clearly announces the climax that is coming:

> I will embrace him with a soldier's arm,
> That he shall shrink under my courtesy.

> (V. ii. 73)

How seriously can we take such a challenge to single combat? Asking this question leads us to think about how politics can be turned into drama. It is clearly not serious politics to settle civil conflict by single combat. The chivalric code would only recognise such conflict as proper if between equals, and no subject is the equal of the prince; and there is the more hard-headed point that the side whose champion lost could not be compelled to accept the verdict. So when the prince issues the challenge the king, after saying that he would be willing to venture his son, adds 'Albeit considerations infinite | Do make against it.' In reality, single combat never was used as a way of avoiding civil war. But whereas battles always have an element of unreality on stage, as the chorus in *Henry V* never tires of reminding us, a fight between two individuals can be intensely dramatic – especially perhaps in the Elizabethan theatre, where many of the audience would have been keenly interested in fencing. Single combats are therefore quite common in Shakespeare – in *Coriolanus, Macbeth, Romeo and Juliet* and *Hamlet*, for instance. But when they form part of a full-scale battle, as is the case here, we are forced into accepting that the winner of the single combat must also be on the winning side. A moment's thought will show us that this need not be the case, but fortunately that does not seem to have worried the contemporary audience, and does not often worry audiences today.

Hal is back among his cronies in Part 2 (though not altogether one of them now), and therefore another reconciliation scene with the king is needed – once again, in the fourth act. This time it is a deathbed scene, but that does not remove the need for reconciliation between father and son – indeed, makes it more necessary. What Shakespeare did was to take a detail which Holinshed records, that the prince, thinking his father already dead, removed the crown which had been placed on his pillow, that the king then awoke, saw that the crown had gone, and called back the prince to reproach him, 'requiring of him what he meant so to misuse himself. The prince with a good audacitie answered; Sir, to mine and all men's judgements, you seemed dead in this world, wherefore I as your next heir apparent, took that as mine own and not as yours.' Holinshed does not indicate whether this reply satisfied the king, but Shakespeare built the episode up into a lengthy exchange between the two of them. Hal's soliloquy as he puts on the crown expands the thought which Holinshed gives him, that this crown with its weight of care is 'my due from thee', but the exchange between him and the king when he comes back has no precedent in Holinshed. Hal now claims that he upbraided the crown for the way it 'fed upon the body of my father', and insists that it did not 'infect my blood with joy'. That is not what we heard the prince say to the crown, and no doubt Shakespeare did not wish us to listen to the same speech twice: presumably this is what the prince said when he was offstage.

The king is wholly satisfied with this answer:

> God put it in thy mind to take it hence,
> That thou mightst win the more thy father's love,
> Pleading so wisely in excuse of it!

> (IV. v. 178)

and then delivers his final speech of advice to the prince.

This scene is the one in which the difficulty of avoiding repetition in a two-part play seems most prominent: having decided to end the two plays very differently – one with a battle, the other with a renunciation – Shakespeare could not avoid the need to repeat, in some way, the reconciliation between father and son. We may feel that in the end it has been solved, but it is impossible to avoid an awareness that there was a difficulty.

THE EPILOGUE

A Shakespeare play usually strikes a note of conclusion in the last speech (as we saw in the case of Part 1) but very few of them have formal epilogues; one of these few is *Henry IV*, Part 2, and we can look at it to ask if it gives us any clues about the original production. Like the epilogue to *As You Like It* it is in prose, but whereas that one seems to have been spoken by the boy who played Rosalind, it is not at all clear who is meant to speak this one. Indeed, it is not clear if this is a single epilogue, or if alternative versions have been bundled together in the text. After the brief introductory sentence there are three paragraphs. The speaker of the first informs us 'what I have to say is of my own making.' Does this mean it was spoken by Shakespeare? That would be odd, since the whole play was of his own making. He remarks that he 'was lately here in the end of a displeasing play, to pray your patience for it, and to promise you a better.' That too could be Shakespeare, or whichever of the actors could be seen as filling a managerial role. It sounds as if it was meant to be spoken on a particular occasion (we do not know which was the displeasing play), perhaps after the first performance; and it ends: 'And so I kneel down before you – but indeed, to pray for the Queen.' That is, he appears to kneel to ask pardon for the displeasing play, then turns it into a formal ending. Kneeling to pray for the queen must, surely, mark the end of the occasion. It looks as if this first paragraph is a complete epilogue, and may later have been replaced by the other two paragraphs.

The second and third paragraphs are about the same length as the first one, and most scholars think they were spoken by a dancer: 'will you command me to use my legs?' – and the final sentence clearly announces a dance. There is no dancing in the play, but no doubt many of the company could dance, and Will Kemp, who usually played the clown, was famous for his dancing. Had he played Falstaff? Certainly the last paragraph is about Falstaff, and it contains two very interesting details. One is the reference to Oldcastle: 'Oldcastle died martyr, and this is not the man'. This sounds like a reminder that the name has been changed, both to reassure the Brooke family and to tell the public to stop calling him Oldcastle. The other is the promise that Falstaff will appear in the next play, which of course he doesn't. This makes it clear that Shakespeare had not yet written *Henry V* (unless we want to believe that the remark was made without his consent by one of the actors as a hint to him!).

Though Falstaff does not appear in *Henry V*, his death is movingly described by the hostess. And what does he die of? 'For anything I know, Falstaff shall die of a sweat, unless already he be killed with your hard opinions': what is this slightly puzzling remark in the epilogue suggesting? 'A sweat' could be the plague, or venereal disease. Falstaff lovers, however, will always insist that he died of a broken heart.

3

After Shakespeare

Once Shakespeare had finished writing his play, and once it had been printed, that was an end of the matter, surely: *Henry IV* was now part of English literature – as it still is. Or are matters not so simple?

We are here concerned with a play, and plays are written not just to be read, but to be performed. In one sense, different performances of the same text are always the same play, in another sense are always a new play. If we stretch the performances over four hundred years and over the whole world, the differences may be very great indeed. The production history of a Shakespeare play, from its own time to the present, tells us that it is always the same yet always different. Actors, directors and theatre audiences have always known this.

This is true, and important, yet there is little one can say about it. There is no point in reading literary criticism of a book we have not read, since criticism offers an interpretation to set beside our own, to point out things we did not notice, or place them in a fresh context for us; it presupposes that our own experience of the work is already present in our minds. Similarly, a discussion of a production we have not seen can tell us little: it may, if it is a review, help us to decide whether to see it, but that is a limited and practical purpose. And to read about a production from the past which neither we nor the person writing it has ever seen will have still less value. For that reason this book will not attempt the impossible task of describing how *Henry IV* was put on the stage over the last four hundred years.

But there is another reason for studying the history of the play over four centuries, one that recent literary theory has given great prominence to. Different people can read the same text differently – not just different individuals, but different ages, and different schools of thought – so that understanding of Shakespeare in the eighteenth century might be very different from that in the twenty-first. This too has long been known, but in the past it would usually have been considered of interest to students of the eighteenth century rather than of Shakespeare; now, however, there are influential critical schools – new historicists and reader-response critics – which reject this distinction, and claim that the meaning of a text is necessarily unstable, because it depends not only on the author's intention but also on the reading community. Indeed, an extreme form of this position maintains that it is determined *solely* by the reading community. For interpreters of this school the study of how different times and places have interpreted *Henry IV* is not an optional extra that we can add to our understanding of the play itself, but is the necessary basis of all understanding.

We know that *Henry IV* was immensely popular during Shakespeare's lifetime. There were seven Quarto editions (that is, small volumes containing one play only) of Part 1 between 1598 and the publication of Shakespeare's complete works in 1623 (only *Richard III* was reprinted so often); and there are several contemporary references to its popularity, from which one thing is very clear: that the popularity was due to Falstaff. Several of these references have survived, and there must have been far more in conversations. Sir Toby Matthew remarked of some English soldiers in 1598 – that is, within a year of the first performance: 'Honour pricks them on, and the world thinks that honour will quickly prick them off again.' Interestingly, quite a number of these early references still call him Oldcastle.

References to Falstaff continue unabated throughout the seventeenth and eighteenth century: thus some commendatory verses on Beaumont and Fletcher in 1647 begin:

> I could praise Heywood now, or tell how long
> Falstaff from cracking nuts hath kept the throng.

Over the centuries, many of the famous Shakespearean actors have played Falstaff or Hotspur (Hal less often): Betterton in the seventeenth century, Quin in the eighteenth (but,interestingly the most famous of eighteenth-century actors, David Garrick, was never a success in the play). *Henry IV* seems to have been rather less popular in Victorian times, at least until Beerbohm Tree's production at the end of the century; but it came into its own in the mid twentieth century, with two productions that have become almost legendary: at the Old Vic in 1945 (Ralph Richardson as Falstaff, Laurence Olivier as Hotspur) and as part of the whole tetralogy at Stratford in 1951 (Richard Burton as Hal, Michael Redgrave as Hotspur, Anthony Quayle as Falstaff). It is not uncommon nowadays to see all four plays done as a series, and in Stratford in 1964–5 both tetralogies (shortened to seven plays) were produced under the general title of 'The Wars of the Roses'.

SHAKESPEARE CRITICISM

Shakespeare criticism (to which this book is a tiny contribution) is now a major literary industry, absorbing the attention of some very distinguished minds – and, inevitably, many more undistinguished ones. It is difficult to date its beginning: probably it began in the form of arguments among the members of the audience emerging from the Globe and discussing the play over their ale. Passing allusions and compliments to Shakespeare gradually grew into more thoughtful essays as Dryden, Addison, Pope and – with greater thoroughness – Samuel Johnson tried to set down their understanding of his greatness. As such discussions became fuller and more philosophical we can see them growing from appreciations in passing to a more systematic, even philosophical, attempt to explain Shakespeare's genius. And as it happens a crucial role in this growth belongs to Falstaff.

'General criticism is as uninstructive as it is easy: Shakespeare deserves to be considered in detail – a task hitherto unattempted.' These fighting words are from *An Essay on the Dramatic Character of Sir John Falstaff*, a book-length study by a government diplomat called Maurice Morgann, published in 1777. It sets out to defend the unusual claim that Falstaff is not a coward: an impossible task, which hardly anyone has found convincing. But the essay is important both because of its eloquent account of Shakespeare's genius, and for its attempt to claim that 'the real character of Falstaff may be different from its apparent one.' That was probably the most serious attempt that had yet been made to treat Shakespeare's characters as having the same kind of existence as real human beings, of whose lives the play gives us only a partial view; and it announces a tradition of criticism which lasted for more than a century, through Hazlitt, Carlyle and Bradley: a tradition that focuses on the characters as the elements out of which a play is made. Real people can command our love in a way that the elements of a play hardly can, so it is not surprising that this tradition has produced two of the most eloquent defences of Falstaff and condemnations of his banishment ever written, by Hazlitt at the beginning of the nineteenth century, and by Bradley at the end. Hazlitt's study of Falstaff, from his *Characters of Shakespeare's Plays* (1817–18) is surely the liveliest and most stylish piece ever written about the old knight: 'his very size floats him out of all his difficulties in a sea of rich conceits.' Bradley's essay is particularly interesting as an extreme example of two elements in Shakespeare criticism that he represents and helped to form: confident assertions about our emotional reaction ('we feel, I think'; 'we stare in astonishment') and about those of the character ('I think he feels a twinge'); and the habit of comparing characters from one play with those from another, as if they all inhabit the same world.

When we turn to the twentieth century, the volume and variety of Shakespeare criticism seems overwhelming. With the inevitable warnings about the danger of oversimplification, I shall attempt to describe the two main currents, under the headings of Historicism and Formalism.

HISTORICISM

'He was not for an age, but for all time.' Ben Jonson's line, in the dedicatory verses to the first folio of 1623, is probably the most famous thing ever said about Shakespeare; and it has echoed down the centuries. Coleridge, writing two hundred years later, said:

> Shakespeare is of no age . . . I believe [he] was not a whit more intelligible in his own day than he is now to an educated man, except

for a few local allusions of no consequence . . . As I said, he is of no age – nor, I may add, of any religion, party or profession. The body and depth of his works came out of the unfathomable depths of his own mind.

The opposite view, that Shakespeare belongs in the England of Elizabeth and James I, and should be studied in relation to the time and place he lived in, can be called historicism. Most critics and readers hold a combination of these two positions, though they often declare their allegiance to only one of them. Academic critics usually know more about history than most people, so it is not surprising that historicism is common in academic circles; and since the mid twentieth century it has probably been the dominant movement in the study of Shakespeare.

E. M. W. Tillyard's study of *Shakespeare's History Plays* was published in 1944, followed by a short book on *The Elizabethan World Picture* in 1945. Their argument was that the picture of civil war and disorder in the histories 'had no meaning apart from a background of order to judge them by', and that this idea of order was not just political but 'was always part of a larger cosmic order', which 'was one of the genuine ruling ideas of the age', essential for understanding its literature. Tillyard's reading of *Henry IV* sees Prince Hal as the hero, 'from the very first a commanding character', takes literally the drawers' remark that he was 'the king of courtesy', and is critical, even dismissive, of both Hotspur and Falstaff: 'From the very beginning' Hotspur 'verges on the ridiculous' and Falstaff 'symbolises disorder'. Falstaff's eventual rejection is clearly necessary.

Tillyard's work is important not so much for his interpretations of particular plays (which are often rather unsubtle) but for its insistence on relating them to Elizabethan ideas of order and degree. He places great emphasis on Ulysses' speech in *Troilus and Cressida* about the importance of order :

> The heavens themselves, the planets, and this centre
> Observe degree, priority and place,
> Insisture, course, proportion, season, form
> Office and custom, in all line of order.

This asserts a cosmic sanction underlying the need to preserve social order and deference:

> How could communities,
> Degrees in schools and brotherhoods in cities,
> Peaceful commerce from dividable shores,
> The primogeniture and due of birth,
> Prerogative of age, crowns, sceptres, laurels,
> But by degree stand in authentic place?

(I. iii. 85-9, 103-8)

Contemporary with Tillyard was John Dover Wilson, who was editing *Henry IV* at the same time as Tillyard was writing, and whose book *The Fortunes of Falstaff* appeared in the year before *Shakespeare's History Plays*. Dover Wilson's title is deliberately ambiguous: he is concerned both with the fortunes of Falstaff in the play, and also with the ups and downs of his critical reception through the centuries. Though he would certainly have claimed that his Falstaff is also Shakespeare's, he is not as rigorously historicist as Tillyard: he enlists the support of anyone who he feels has understood Falstaff correctly, and his main ally is Samuel Johnson, writing a century and a half after Shakespeare.

There is an obvious objection to interpreting Shakespeare's Histories by means of Tudor political doctrine: that it reduces the work of a great dramatist to the level of (often rather crude) political propaganda. This position is stated very fully and convincingly by Robert Ornstein in his book on Shakespeare's Histories, *A Kingdom for a Stage* (1972). Quoting Prince Hal in his support, Ornstein suggests that the Elizabethan dramatists would not have considered themselves 'blessed fellows' to think 'the way everybody thinks'. Ornstein points out that the chronicles which Tillyard invokes so authoritatively were 'a hodgepodge of significant and trivial facts, of shrewd judgements and fantastic opinions, eclectically gathered and often uncritically repeated.' He claims that the Elizabethans may seem to us 'simpler and more transparent than do our contemporaries because we know less about the diversity, contradictions, shadings and facets of their beliefs.' Ornstein's sceptical common sense has no particular ideological purpose behind it, but a sentence like this does anticipate the very different historicism that has now become prominent. The critical school known as new historicism in America, and its English cousin, cultural materialism, also relate Shakespeare to the ideas of his

59

own time, and they are sceptical of eternal values and of the idea that great literature transcends, or breaks free of, its age. But they often attack Tillyard explicitly, as representing the critical tradition they are setting out to reject. What then is the difference between the new and the old historicism?

Most important is their picture of sixteenth-century society, which new historicism sees as riven by conflicts and fissures, so that the world picture of an ordered hierarchical system of 'degree, priority and place' should be seen not as a statement of what everyone believed, but as an attempt – even, at times, a desperate attempt – to impose control. Why, we could ask, were the clergy obliged, Sunday after Sunday, to preach the necessity of obedience and the wickedness of rebellion? Is it not a sign of the presence of *dis*obedience, of the danger that royal authority is not accepted as unquestioningly as desired? New historicists and cultural materialists therefore see the idea of order as a weapon in the conflict between the haves and the have-nots, as 'those beliefs and practices which work to legitimate the social order', in the words of Dollimore and Sinfield – who then go on to reveal their own radical position by asserting that 'the principal strategy of ideology is to legitimate inequality and exploitation by representing the social order which perpetuates these things as immutable and unalterable – as decreed by God or simply natural.' This is not so much a denial of Tillyard's Elizabethan world picture as a more cynical account of its political function.

There is an interesting contrast here with Stephen Greenblatt, probably the leading figure of the new historicism: for him this 'legitimation' is much less obviously successful. Greenblatt suggests that 2 *Henry IV* 'seems to be testing and confirming an extremely dark and disturbing hypothesis about the nature of monarchical power in England: that its moral authority rests upon a hypocrisy so deep that the hypocrites themselves believe it.' Though Greenblatt accepts the radical/cynical concept of ideology, he does not accept the simplistic radical thesis of literature as serving a straightforward ideological function.

There is another important aspect of new historicism: its refusal to privilege literature (this use of 'privilege' as a verb is a favourite locution of cultural materialism: it implies a rejection of the usual distinction between the highbrow and the popular, and suggests that the idea of a literary canon has a not altogether legitimate function, bestowing unwarranted privilege on the highbrow). Since the medium of literature is language, we can start by thinking about the relation between the language of literature and the socially rooted language in which we conduct our everyday affairs. For Paul Valéry, writing in the early twentieth century, poetry was an attempt to construct 'a language within the language'. He envied the musician who could do this effortlessly, since music belongs to the special world of sound, not the everyday world of noise. The poet, on the other hand, has nothing to compose with but the public voice, the language of newspapers and everyday speech, and so poetry, in order to recapture its birthright, to emulate music, has to construct its own language. Of course this ideal has not always been accepted by poets: we have only to think of Wordsworth's insistence that poetry should reject poetic diction and be in 'the real language of men' – and it was certainly not accepted by the Shakespeare who created Falstaff. More relevant to our immediate purpose, it is not accepted by critics who wish to relate the language of literature to the language of ordinary social – and political – transactions. And so the new historicist looks at non-literary texts not just for background information, but in order to find in them the same tensions and conflicts that he finds in the most complex poetry.

Greenblatt's historical method is a drastic example of this. He takes a nugget of history – an anecdote from a memoir, a sermon or a travel narrative, a speculation from a book about magic – and asks what it tells us about power relations in the society; then he turns to a literary or dramatic text, and asks much the same questions about it, thus establishing his claim that there is nothing privileged or autonomous about works of art: they participate, as do all texts, in the circulation of social energy that is continually going on. The examples that Greenblatt chooses range from the merely eccentric to the brilliant. In his essay 'Invisible Bullets', he relates Shakespeare's history plays to Harriot's *Brief and True Account of the New Found Land of Virginia*, a text which has nothing to do with English history but is chosen in order to explore how far orthodox political assertions of the need for authority also contain subversion. (The possible pun *contain* in the sense of 'include' and in the sense of 'control' seems made for Greenblatt!) One of his most compelling parallels is that between the Renaissance artist and the Renaissance monarch. The ambivalence of the creative act, by which the text appears to be the spontaneous production of an autonomous self while at the same time expressing 'complex networks of despondency and fear', corresponds to the ambivalence of the prince's power, which is suppose to emanate from him directly and subdue society to his will, whereas we know (and at some level the Elizabethans knew) that it is largely a collective invention.

Since new historicism is heavily influenced by recent literary theories that often describe themselves as 'anti-humanist', it is worth adding that Greenblatt has also written a warmly human life of Shakespeare, which proposes a personal origin for much of what appears in the plays, and includes the suggestion that the rejection of Falstaff may draw on Shakespeare's own embarrassed encounters with drunkenness, perhaps including that of his father: 'It is difficult to register the overwhelming power and pathos of the relationship between Hal and Falstaff without sensing some unusually intimate and personal energy'. This touching suggestion could come from almost any nineteenth-century critic in the Romantic tradition.

Of course new historicism has not gone unchallenged, and the most carefully documented attack it has received (and one of the fiercest) is Brian Vickers' book *Appropriating Shakespeare*. If we can imagine Tillyard returning from the dead, with a sophisticated awareness of the modern critical scene, and defending his reading of Shakespeare, the result might be something like this book, which combines Tillyard's traditionally historical reading of Shakespeare with a lively attempt to situate the new historicists themselves historically, as disillusioned liberals, critical of modern American foreign policy. (There may be no better way of introducing oneself to modern critical controversy about *Henry IV* than to read 'Invisible Bullets' along with Chapter 4, section V (pages 257–67) of Vickers' book.)

The view of Shakespeare propounded by the cultural materialists is probably best studied in two very influential collections of essays, both published in 1985: *Political Shakespeare*, edited by Jonathan Dollimore and Alan Sinfield, and *Alternative Shakespeares*, edited by John Drakakis. The approach is described

62

by Dollimore and Sinfield as based on historical context (undermining 'the transcendent significance traditionally accorded to the literary text'), theoretical method (deriving from Marxism, post-structuralism and the work of Foucault), political commitment (radical) and textual analysis. The coherent subject of traditional humanism is replaced by the decentred subject, and transcendent truths by ideological positions.

In applying their approach to Shakespeare's history plays, Dollimore and Sinfield deal more with *Henry V* than *Henry IV*, but their analysis can easily be broadened, indeed it is broadened by them. Their observation that for a play about national unity, *Henry V* is 'obsessively preoccupied with insurrection' obviously applies to *Henry IV* as well; though their very interesting discussion of the conspiracy in *Henry V*, pointing out that we are never told what its aims were, so that the conspirators are presented as 'motivated by greed and incomprehensible evil', does suggest a contrast with *Henry IV*, where the rebels are treated at much greater length – and this could be used to argue that *Henry V* presents a cruder view of politics than *Henry IV* does.

An extreme example of cultural materialism is Graham Holderness's book *Shakespeare's History*, also published in 1985. Some careful criticism of the history plays is set in an ideological framework which describes the Elizabethan theatres as 'purpose-built playhouses run entirely on profitable lines', claiming that they disclose 'with absolute clarity the fact that the players were selling a commodity for cash', and sees Elizabethan drama 'as a systematically constructed ideology of national unity designed to confirm the state's authority'. Holderness's criticism of Tillyard is particularly fierce, claiming that Tillyard's real interest is not in history but in his own time, 'masking its essential conservatism in an impenetrable disguise of academic scholarship'.

It might seem odd that new historicism and cultural materialism should choose Tillyard as one of their main targets when arguing for their method of interpreting Shakespeare: was he not a historicist too? Partly this can be explained by the natural tendency of radical critics to attack their immediate predecessors, those who look like allies but did not go far enough; and it also indicates their suspicion that Tillyard is not really a historicist, that he is sneaking in his own conservative stance under the guise of the non-political. I think this is unfair on Tillyard: it is quite difficult to discover from his criticism what Tillyard's own political opinions were, or even if he had any. But this defence is not altogether to his credit: his application of the ideas of order and degree to Elizabethan literature is more or less mechanical, and never generates the kind of complex exploration that shows a critic at his most incisive – and at his most individual. The accusation could, however, be applied with more justice to Dover Wilson, who does not mind giving us glimpses of his dislike of much in early twentieth-century culture (pacifism and 'starved intellectuals') and his own admiration for 'authority based on and working through a carefully preserved gradation of rank'.

Though new historicists castigate the old historicists because they use Shakespeare to support a conservative view of society, this is not meant to suggest that Shakespeare criticism should avoid dealing with our own times: on the contrary, they are as intensely concerned with the political situation from which Shakespeare is read as with the situation in which he wrote. To illustrate this I will cite Lisa Jardine's introduction to her lively and argumentative book *Reading Shakespeare Historically*. In describing the development of her thinking about Shakespeare, she finds it necessary to describe not only the way 'social historians and social anthropologists' have given us 'an entirely unexpected, vivid version of everyday life in the early modern period', but also the impact of political conflicts in the late twentieth century, the use made of Shakespeare by modern politicians, and the intellectual controversies among modern Shakespeare scholars at their 'ground-breaking' conferences. Historicism, that is, does not here mean emerging from modern thought to enter that of the sixteenth century, but exploring ways in which they illuminate each other.

This has produced one fascinating paradox. Radical critics today will naturally be on the hunt for radicalism in earlier texts: so whereas it was orthodox among Shakespeare critics in the mid twentieth century to speak of the conservative ideology underlying his plays, it is now standard practice to read them as sceptical interrogations of order and degree. Unorthodoxy has become the new orthodoxy.

To illustrate fully the shifts in the way Shakespeare's Histories are read would of course require a full study of modern criticism, and the bibliography offers suggestions for how this could be done; but to give a glimpse of how such shifts affect our way of looking at particular details, we can take a single metaphor. When Hal meets his father in Part 1 he promises, as we have seen, to redeem himself by fighting Percy:

> Percy is but my factor, good my lord,
> To engross up glorious deeds on my behalf,
> And I will call him to so strict account
> That he shall render every glory up. . . . .
> Or I will tear the reckoning from his heart.
>
> (III. ii. 147)

A factor is an agent, and the sustained metaphor here is taken from commerce: 'engross', 'account', 'render' and 'reckoning' are all commercial terms. Hal claims Percy (without knowing it) has been accumulating honour not for himself, but on behalf of the prince. And so Phyllis Rackin seizes on the metaphor to claim that the use of these terms 'reduces the chivalric battle to a closely calculated financial transaction'.

Would an Elizabethan reader, noticing the metaphor, have read it this way? What Rackin has done (and in this her comment is typical of much recent criticism) is to treat the metaphor as if the choice of vehicle was ideologically significant. A metaphor or a simile can be analysed into 'tenor' and 'vehicle': if we say that a secret has leaked out, or that an argument has collapsed like a house of cards, we are comparing the secret (tenor) to water in a container (vehicle), or the argument (tenor) to a house of cards (vehicle); but that need not imply that the secret can evaporate or that the argument was used for gambling, because the comparison is limited to the one aspect of the vehicle. Now it was quite common, in Elizabethan poetry, to use similes and metaphors from trade: Edmund Spenser built a whole sonnet, written as a compliment to his mistress, on a comparison between her beauty and 'the world's riches' which merchants bring back from the Indies. Does such an image imply a commercial aspect to love? We cannot assume this: it would reduce the inventiveness of poets to a helpless enslavement to ideology. In Spenser's case such an implication

65

is almost certainly not there, and it seems unlikely Shakespeare is inviting us to see the relation between Hal and Percy as being in any wider sense commercial.

Would we expect cultural materialists and new historicists to be at their best when writing about Shakespeare's Histories? Common sense might say yes, since a concern with power, and a tendency to see issues politically, would seem to fit best with the study of Shakespeare's most explicitly political plays. But neither these critics nor their opponents are likely to accept this view. A cultural materialist, especially if a follower of Foucault, will tend to see questions of power everywhere, not only in the explicitly political; the eclectic critic who is sceptical of allegiance to a particular school is likely to think that the deepest insights come from the critic with the subtlest and most brilliant mind, the one who can make us catch our breath, irrespective of what school he belongs to, or how well his school fits the subject of particular plays. To illustrate this, I will (briefly) anticipate the coming discussion of William Empson, probably the most brilliant (though certainly not the most reliable) Shakespeare critic there has ever been. He quotes from Mistress Quickly's tearfully indulgent remarks on Falstaff: 'Well, fare thee well; I have known thee these twenty-nine years, come peascod time, but an honester and truer hearted man – well, fare thee well.' (II. iv. 377) This comes in Empson's discussion of the word 'honest', which explores how the range of meanings of the word – sincerity, financial probity, deserving of honour, cynicism, and (only in English) telling truth – illustrates changing moral ideas in European history. He then says: 'Here "true-hearted" lets *honest* mean a good deal, whether as "faithful to friends" or in some more obscure way as "with the right kind of feelings", ready to share his pleasures perhaps. The muddle of her ideas is made actively pathetic.' Empson shared many of the political views of the cultural materialists, but the value of commentary like this seems quite independent of his own political position.

FORMALISM AND AMBIGUITY

Historicists look outward, relating the work to its social context, and therefore contrast with those critics who look into the work itself, and study it by examining the structure and the tensions, and especially the complexities of its language. The usual term applied to such critics, especially by their opponents, is 'formalist'; sometimes, adapting a term from German, they are called 'work-immanent' critics. It might seem obvious that there is a place for both these approaches, but in the world of literary theory they have often been bitter opponents.

For the formalist, the value of a literary work lies not in what it says (its paraphrasable content) but in the particularities of its way of saying it. For Cleanth Brooks, perhaps the leading American formalist of the mid twentieth century, a poem was a 'well-wrought urn'; this is the title of his most famous book, and its chapter on Shakespeare, which deals with *Macbeth*, is called 'The Naked Babe and the Cloak of Manliness': an announcement that what is important about the play is not what it says, about kingship or tyranny or military prowess, but its pattern of imagery.

Close attention to the details of the language dominated Shakespeare criticism during the mid and later twentieth century. It seemed obvious to the critics who practised it that this was the proper way to study Shakespeare, since it was an attempt to explore what matters most not only in his plays but in all poetry, the mastery of language. But if we look first at one of the most influential of such critics, G. Wilson Knight, we can see that the term 'formalist' can be rather misleading, since he most certainly tried to look out from the work – not however to its social context, but to an almost mystical concern with its message, the light it throws on human nature and the meaning of life. And Wilson Knight's most famous work, *The Wheel of Fire* (1930), deals mostly with the tragedies: it is even arguable that formalist criticism is more suited to tragedy than to either comedy or history.

At one extreme, the formalist treats Shakespeare's plays as a single work, tracing the patterns of imagery without much bothering to distinguish one play from another. Thus when Hotspur complains about Bolingbroke

> Why, what a candy deal of courtesy
> This fawning greyhound then did proffer me,

(II. iv. 377)

Edward Armstrong points out parallels with passages from half a dozen other plays in which dogs and candy are associated with flattery and untrustworthiness. The most famous such studies are *Leading Motives in the Imagery of Shakespeare's Tragedies* (1930) and *Shakespeare's Iterative Imagery* (1931) by Caroline Spurgeon, *The Development of Shakespeare's Imagery* by W. H. Clemen, and *Shakespeare's Imagination* by Edward Armstrong (1963).

Teasing out the effects produced by the complexities of the language leads naturally to a keen awareness of the complexities and ambiguities of words, so that the 'formalist' critics can be linked to a figure who was certainly not a formalist. William Empson, eccentric, original, often difficult, was once described as 'the wisest fool in Christendom', and he wrote at length on *Henry IV*.

Empson's first book, *Seven Types of Ambiguity* (1930) announces its interest in wordplay by the title; and his greatest book, *The Structure of Complex Words,* explores what he calls the 'equations' which a poem or play sets up between the different meanings of its key words. A complex word is not a word like 'aerodynamics' or 'psycho-analysis', which denote a difficult concept but are quite simple *as words*; it is a word that has a wide range of meanings, and a rich poem will explore it by suggesting how one of its meanings might interact with another. Thus *Othello* is discussed by exploring how the word *honest* is used, and *King Lear* through the word *fool*. When Hotspur in his dying speech refers to life as 'Time's fool', Empson focuses on the ambiguity: that 'time makes us clowns, but we in our turn mock at time.'

Empson twice discussed *Henry IV* at length: in *Some Versions of Pastoral* (1935) and in a long essay on Falstaff, printed in his posthumous *Essays on Shakespeare* (1986). Much of the latter takes the form of a response to Dover Wilson, picking up many of his suggestions about how the play should be staged. Dover Wilson differed from other historical critics by his keen interest in the staging of the plays, and much of his account of Falstaff consists of lively suggestions of how the scenes should be performed. Thus the episode in which Prince Hal takes the crown from his father's pillow is described like this:

He falls to his knees by the dead man, as he supposes him to be, and remains a moment before walking out of the room, shaken with sobs and as in a dream; the crown, now forgotten, still upon his head.'

This fits with Dover Wilson's conception of the prince, whom, like Tillyard, he considers a wholly admirable character, and it would be a very powerful way to perform this scene. But it is not the only way. Theatrically-centred critics are always conscious of how productions can differ, and how not only individual directors but also changing historical circumstances lead to the enormous variety of stage representation. Dover Wilson's interest in the theatre was certainly genuine, but when combined with his (often dogmatic) historicism, it leads him to write as if there is only one right way to do a scene. In contrast to this, Empson insists on the notion of dramatic ambiguity. This is rather different from the verbal ambiguity that he usually explores, since it is explained in social rather than verbal terms, as the variety of views present in the audience, and the probability that they will not all respond to a scene in the same way.

As a simple example we can look at the Gadshill robbery, the very first episode in the sub-plot. When Poins comes in with the news that there will be pilgrims 'with rich offerings' and travellers 'with fat purses' riding at Gads Hill the next morning, Falstaff asks the prince if he will join in the plan to rob them; Hal replies 'Who I? Rob? I a thief? Not I, by my faith.' The teasing which Hal has already indulged in, and this (surely) over emphatic language, suggest that this is likely to be mock indignation, but Dover Wilson insists that it is genuine: 'the proposal . . . is received at first with something like indignation, even with a touch of haughtiness, and only consented to when Poins intimates, by nods and winks behind Falstaff's back, that he is planning to make a practical joke of it.' This is an extreme example of Dover Wilson's habit of claiming that there is one right way of producing the scene, and Empson responds by pointing out that 'the nods and winks are invented by the critic, of course (and printed in his text of the play)'. He then adds that they are 'plausible enough' and states his case for dramatic ambiguity: 'the balance is still being kept: you can decide with relief that surely after this he can't be a thief, or you can feel, if you prefer, he has practically admitted that for the present he is one.' Ambiguity in poetry, especially when discovered by

Empson, often produces complicated and controversial readings; ambiguity in drama often sounds like sheer common sense, since audiences are not uniform.

FEMINIST CRITICISM

If we were concerned to give a full picture of modern Shakespeare criticism, there should now be a section on feminism, since feminist readings of Shakespeare are now among the most influential in academic study. But the four plays of the second tetralogy happen to be those on which feminism has least to say, since there are no prominent female characters in them – fewer even than in the earlier tetralogy, in which both Joan of Arc and Queen Margaret are given a prominence that no woman attains in the later histories. Phyllis Rackin points out that Glendower's daughter represents nothing but distraction from the serious business of English politics: she speaks only Welsh, so cannot say anything comprehensible to the audience, and her sole function is to offer sexual delight as a distraction from serious politics. Mortimer, who should be a serious political figure, is reduced by her to a submissive husband. (It has even been suggested that the way new historicists concentrate on the second tetralogy is evidence of their hostility to feminist criticism.)

There is however one ingenious way in which a feminist reading of *Henry IV* can be offered, and has been by Valerie Traub: that is to feminise Falstaff. Traub's argument is not easy to summarise simply, since it is heavily dependent on psychoanalytic theory, Lacanian rather than directly Freudian, and makes great use of Bakhtin, Foucault and other recent theorists. Its central claim is that Falstaff offers a version of the Bakhtinian 'grotesque body', which is normally seen as female: Falstaff's 'somatic iconography metonymically positions him as the fantasised pre-Oedipal maternal.' When Hal declares to his father that by fighting with Percy he will 'wear a garment all of blood | And stain my favours in a bloody mask', Traub sees the blood as 'the blood of birth, that, when washed away, will scour off the filth of his maternal associations'. This small example points to the central strategy of such a critical approach, its brushing aside of the literal: if Shakespeare's lines are read in the light of psychoanalytic theory, they can constantly be made to yield symbolic meanings quite different from what they actually say, and the fact that Falstaff is not actually a woman becomes unimportant.

.   .   .

By dividing the discussion into two main sections, the play itself and its changing interpretation, this book has offered two different ways of seeing a Shakespeare play: as something we experience direct, and as something whose understanding is constituted by the changing interpretations that have been offered of it. In its extreme form, as espoused by some reader-response criticism, this can lead to the claim that the entire meaning of a text is determined by its interpreters. As well as the major task of helping you to understand *Henry IV,* this book may serve the further task of helping you to choose between – or find a satisfactory blend of – these two positions.

Bibliography

EDITIONS OF *HENRY IV*

Does it matter what edition of *Henry IV* we use? We cannot read Shakespeare today without the help of an editor. A commentary such as the present book is a discussion of Shakespeare's text and the issues it raises in the mind of the modern reader or theatre-goer. This presupposes that we know what Shakespeare's text is; but in many ways we don't. Textual scholarship is the attempt to find out, and the way to do this is to understand what happened to his words once he had written them.

Shakespeare handed them to the company so that the play could be put on stage, and then his words were mauled about by scribes, actors, censors and printers. If we think of Shakespeare as an autonomous writer, then we shall try to scrape away all this interference, and find out what he originally wrote. But if we think of him as a man of the theatre, our aim will be slightly different: to find what the Elizabethan public saw when they went to the theatre, and this may not be what he first wrote. Playwrights often make changes or accept suggestions while a play is being put on stage.

In recent years there has been a shift among editors, away from the former (more literary) conception of what our text should be, to a more theatrical conception of what it ended up as in the theatre. This is the policy of the recent one-volume Oxford edition of the complete works, whose most controversial decision was to restore the name Oldcastle instead of Falstaff, on the grounds that that was what Shakespeare originally wrote and that the change was imposed on him. This has, of course, the objection that he then has a different name in the second part, where he was always called Falstaff. But on the whole, fortunately, the two parts of *Henry IV* (unlike, for instance, *Hamlet* or *King Lear*) do not raise many serious textual problems, and the various modern editions do not, in consequence, differ greatly from one another in their text. The most important modern one-volume editions are:

The Oxford Shakespeare (Oxford University Press). Part 1 edited by David Bevington (1987), Part 2 edited by René Weiss (1998).
The Arden Shakespeare (Methuen). Both parts edited by Arthur Humphreys (1960 and 1966). Humphreys' edition of Part I has now been replaced by David Scott Kazan's fresh edition (2002) but his edition of Part II (reprinted in 2005) is still available.
The New Cambridge Shakespeare. Part I edited by Herbert and Judith Weil (1997), Part II edited by Giorgio Melchiori (1989).
The Penguin Shakespeare. Both parts edited by Peter Davison (1968 and 1977); Davison's straightforward and helpful introductions have now been replaced with fresh essays by Charles Edelman and Adrian Poole.

The Arden is the fullest and most elaborately edited modern edition of Shakespeare, especially in its revised form, discussing historical and textual questions in great detail: a single volume can run to over 300 pages, and at times a rivulet of text seems to cross a meadow of commentary. Excellent for thorough study, awkward for reading or performing.

The Oxford, Arden and (especially) New Cambridge Shakespeare are excellently illustrated with pictures of productions.

Quotations in this book are taken from the Penguin Shakespeare, the most widely-used and convenient edition.

CRITICISM

(The critics marked with an asterisk are discussed in the survey of criticism in Part 3.)

Books

*Tillyard, E. M. W.: *Shakespeare's History Plays* (London: Chatto & Windus, 1944).
Campbell, Lily B.: *Shakespeare's Histories: Mirrors of Elizabethan Policy* (San Marino, Calif.: Huntingdon Library, 1947). An 'old historicist', similar to Tillyard.
Ribner, Irving: *The English History Play in the Age of Shakespeare*

(Princeton: Princeton University Press, 1957).

Barber, C. L.: *Shakespeare's Festive Comedy* (Princeton: Princeton University Press, 1959). This brilliant book relates drama to the popular tradition of festival. The chapter on *Henry IV* deals with rule and misrule, and sees the play as blocking off irony by its ending.

*Ornstein, Robert: *A Kingdom for a Stage: The Achievement of Shakespeare's History Plays* (Cambridge, Mass.: Harvard University Press, 1972).

*Drakakis, John (ed.): *Alternative Shakespeares* (London: Methuen, 1985).

*Dollimore, Jonathan and Alan Sinfield (eds): *Political Shakespeare: New Essays in Cultural Materialism* (Manchester: Manchester University Press, 1985).

*Holderness, Graham: *Shakespeare's History* (Dublin: Gill & Macmillan, 1985).

———— *Shakespeare: The Historie* (Basingstoke: Macmillan Press, 2000).

Leggatt, Alexander: *Shakespeare's Political Drama* (London: Routledge, 1988). The two genres (Comedy and History) coexist peacefully for much of the play; at the ending. Comedy finally steps into the path of History, and is crushed.

*Rackin, Phyllis: *Stages of History: Shakespeare's English Chronicle* (Ithaca, NY: Cornell University Press, 1990).

*Traub, Valerie: *Desire & Anxiety: Circulations of Sexuality in Shakespearean Drama* (London: Routledge, 1992).

*Vickers, Brian: *Appropriating Shakespeare: Contemporary Critical Quarrels* (New Haven: Yale University Press, 1993).

*Jardine, Lisa: *Reading Shakespeare Historically* (London: Routledge, 1996).

Bate, Jonathan: *The Genius of Shakespeare* (London: Picador, 1997). One of the best general books on Shakespeare. Its chapter on 'The National Poet' discusses the Histories, and is very indulgent to Falstaff.

Howard, Jean E. and Phyllis Rackin: *Engendering a Nation: A Feminist Account of Shakespeare's English Histories* (London: Routledge, 1997).

Kermode, Frank: *Shakespeare's Language* (London: Penguin 2000). The brief section on *Henry IV* points out that it (and several plays written shortly after it) uses much more prose than Shakespeare's earlier work, and that Hotspur, the denouncer of poetry, actually has 'the strongest lines, the most intense metaphors'.

The Cambridge Companion to Shakespeare's History Plays, ed. Michael Hattaway (Cambridge: Cambridge University Press, 2002). Particularly valuable for Hattaway's introduction.

Articles

(A very brief selection from the innumerable articles on the plays.)

*Bradley, A. C.: 'The Rejection of Falstaff', in *Oxford Lectures on Poetry*

(1909); often reprinted.

Knights, L. C.: 'Time's Subjects: The Sonnets and *King Henry IV, Part II* in *Some Shakespearean Themes* (London: Chatto & Windus, 1960).

Auden, W. H.: 'The Prince's Dog' in *The Dyer's Hand* (London: Faber & Faber, 1963). 'Falstaff never really does anything, but he never stops talking, so that the impression he makes on the audience is not that of idleness but of infinite energy. He radiates happiness as Hal radiates power, and this . . . untiring devotion to making others laugh becomes a comic image for a love which is absolutely self-giving.'

Burckhardt, Sigurd: ' "Swoll'n with Some Other Grief": Shakespeare's Prince Hal Trilogy' in *Shakespearean Meanings* (Princeton: Princeton University Press, 1968). Contrasts the two methods of succession, primogeniture and combat. The first is officially sanctioned and frequently asserted, but not often confirmed by the action; the second could be viewed as a way of leaving the outcome to God. Neither model seems totally acceptable, so that Shakespeare 'operates with two mutually inconsistent and severally inadequate models'.

Worden, Blair: 'Shakespeare and Politics' in *Shakespeare Survey* 44 (1991). 'Tillyard and others have taught us much about what Tudor Englishmen were told to think of rebellion, but we know less about what they did think.'

Hawkes, Terence: 'Bryn Glas' in *Post-Colonial Shakespeares* ed. Ania Loomba and Martin Orkin (London: Routledge, 1998). The title refers to the battle of Pilleth, at which the Welsh defeated the English and Edmund Mortimer was captured; it also refers to Derrida's *Glas*, which provocatively juxtaposes a rational text by Hegel with the subversive and irrational writings of Jean Genet. Hawkes similarly tries to undermine English domination of British culture by presenting Welsh as subversive and polysemous.

Index

Recent and
Forthcoming Titles
in the
New Series of

WRITERS AND
THEIR WORK

"...this series promises to outshine its own
previously high reputation."
Times Higher Education Supplement

"...will build into a fine multi-volume critical
encyclopaedia of English literature."
Library Review & Reference Review

"...Excellent, informative, readable, and recommended."
NATE News

"written by outstanding contemporary critics,
whose expertise is flavoured by unashamed enthusiasm for
their subjects and the series' diverse aspirations."
Times Educational Supplement

"A useful and timely addition to the ranks of the lit crit and
reviews genre. Written in an accessible and authoritative style."
Library Association Record

RECENT & FORTHCOMING TITLES

Title	Author
Chinua Achebe	Nahem Yousaf
Peter Ackroyd	Susana Onega
Fleur Adcock	Janet Wilson
Kingsley Amis	Richard Bradford
Anglo-Saxon Verse	Graham Holderness
Antony and Cleopatra 2/e	Ken Parker
Matthew Arnold	Kate Campbell
As You Like It	Penny Gay
Margaret Atwood	Marion Wynne-Davies
W. H. Auden	Stan Smith
Jane Austen	Robert Miles
Alan Ayckbourn	Michael Holt
J. G. Ballard	Michel Delville
Pat Barker	Sharon Monteith
Djuna Barnes	Deborah Parsons
Julian Barnes	Matthew Pateman
Samuel Beckett	Sinead Mooney
Aphra Behn 2/e	S. J. Wiseman
John Betjeman	Dennis Brown
William Blake	Steven Vine
Edward Bond	Michael Mangan
Anne Brontë	Betty Jay
Emily Brontë	Stevie Davies
Robert Browning	John Woolford
Robert Burns	Gerard Carruthers
A. S. Byatt	Richard Todd
Byron	Drummond Bone
Caroline Drama	Julie Sanders
Angela Carter 2/e	Lorna Sage
Bruce Chatwin	Kerry Featherstone
Geoffrey Chaucer	Steve Ellis
Children's Literature	Kimberley Reynolds
Caryl Churchill 2/e	Elaine Aston
John Clare	John Lucas
Arthur Hugh Clough	John Schad
S. T. Coleridge	Stephen Bygrave
Joseph Conrad	Cedric Watts
Coriolanus	Anita Pacheco
Stephen Crane	Kevin Hayes
Crime Fiction	Martin Priestman
Anita Desai	Elaine Ho
Shashi Deshpande	Armrita Bhalla
Charles Dickens	Rod Mengham
John Donne	Stevie Davies
Margaret Drabble	Glenda Leeming
John Dryden	David Hopkins
Carol Ann Duffy 2/e	Deryn Rees Jones
Douglas Dunn	David Kennedy
Early Modern Sonneteers	Michael Spiller
George Eliot	Josephine McDonagh
T. S. Eliot	Colin MacCabe
English Translators of Homer	Simeon Underwood

RECENT & FORTHCOMING TITLES

Title	Author
J. G. Farrell	John McLeod
Henry Fielding	Jenny Uglow
Veronica Forrest-Thomson – Language Poetry	Alison Mark
E. M. Forster	Nicholas Royle
John Fowles	William Stephenson
Brian Friel	Geraldine Higgins
Athol Fugard	Dennis Walder
Elizabeth Gaskell	Kate Flint
The *Gawain*-Poet	John Burrow
The Georgian Poets	Rennie Parker
William Golding 2/e	Kevin McCarron
Graham Greene	Peter Mudford
Neil M. Gunn	J. B. Pick
Ivor Gurney	John Lucas
Hamlet 2/e	Ann Thompson & Neil Taylor
Thomas Hardy 2/e	Peter Widdowson
Tony Harrison	Joe Kelleher
William Hazlitt	J. B. Priestley; R. L. Brett (intro. by Michael Foot)
Seamus Heaney 2/e	Andrew Murphy
George Herbert	T.S. Eliot (intro. by Peter Porter)
Geoffrey Hill	Andrew Roberts
Gerard Manley Hopkins	Daniel Brown
Ted Hughes	Susan Bassnett
Henrik Ibsen 2/e	Sally Ledger
Kazuo Ishiguro 2/e	Cynthia Wong
Henry James – The Later Writing	Barbara Hardy
James Joyce 2/e	Steven Connor
Julius Caesar	Mary Hamer
Franz Kafka	Michael Wood
John Keats	Kelvin Everest
James Kelman	Gustav Klaus
Rudyard Kipling	Jan Montefiore
Hanif Kureishi	Ruvani Ranasinha
Samuel Johnson	Liz Bellamy
William Langland: *Piers Plowman*	Claire Marshall
King Lear	Terence Hawkes
Philip Larkin 2/e	Laurence Lerner
D. H. Lawrence	Linda Ruth Williams
Doris Lessing	Elizabeth Maslen
C. S. Lewis	William Gray
Wyndham Lewis and Modernism	Andrzej Gasiorek
David Lodge	Bernard Bergonzi
Macbeth	Kate McLuskie
Louis MacNeice & Poetry of 1930s	Richard D. Brown
Katherine Mansfield	Andrew Bennett
Christopher Marlowe	Thomas Healy
Andrew Marvell	Annabel Patterson
Ian McEwan 2/e	Kiernan Ryan
Measure for Measure	Kate Chedgzoy
The Merchant of Venice	Warren Chernaik
Middleton and His Collaborators	Hutchings & Bromham
A Midsummer Night's Dream	Helen Hackett

RECENT & FORTHCOMING TITLES

TITLES IN PREPARATION

Title	Author
Ama Ata Aidoo	*Nana Wilson-Tagoe*
Martin Amis	*Nicholas Bentley*
John Banville	*Peter Dempsey*
Elizabeth Barrett Browning	*Simon Avery*
Black British Writers	*Deidre Osborne*
Charlotte Brontë	*Stevie Davies*
Basil Bunting	*Martin Stannard*
John Bunyan	*Tamsin Spargoe*
Margaret Cavendish	*Kate Lilly*
Cymbeline	*Peter Swaab*
Charles Darwin	*Rick Rylance*
David Edgar	*Peter Boxall*
Nadine Gordimer	*Lewis Nkosi*
Geoffrey Grigson	*R. M. Healey*
David Hare	*Jeremy Ridgman*
Bessie Head	*Dorothy Driver*
The Imagist Poets	*Andrew Thacker*
Ben Jonson	*Anthony Johnson*
A. L. Kennedy	*Dorothy McMillan*
Jack Kerouac	*Michael Hrebebiak*
Jamaica Kincaid	*Susheila Nasta*
Vernon Lee	*Sandeep Kandola*
Rosamond Lehmann	*Judy Simon*
Una Marson & Louise Bennett	*Alison Donnell*
Norman MacCaig	*Alasdair Macrae*
Toni Morrison	*Rebecca Ferguson*
Much Ado About Nothing	*John Wilders*
R. K. Narayan	*Shirley Chew*
Ngugi wa Thiong'o	*Brendon Nicholls*
Religious Poets of the 17th Century	*Helen Wilcox*
Samuel Richardson	*David Deeming*
Michèle Roberts	*Edith Frampton*
Ruskin & Pre-Raphaelite Poetry	*Lindsay Smith*
Olive Schreiner	*Carolyn Burdett*
Sam Selvon	*Ramchand & Salick*
Olive Senior	*Denise de Caires Narain*
Mary Shelley	*Catherine Sharrock*
Charlotte Smith & Helen Williams	*Angela Keane*
R. L. Stevenson	*David Robb*
Tom Stoppard	*Nicholas Cadden*
David Storey	*George Hyde*
Dylan Thomas	*Chris Wiggington*
Three Avant Garde Poets	*Peter Middleton*
Twelfth Night	*Michael Dobson*
Victorian Sages	*Gavin Budge*
Derek Walcott	*Stephen Regan*
Jeanette Winterson	*Gina Vitello*
Women's Poetry at the Fin de Siècle	*Anna Vadillo*
William Wordsworth	*Nicola Trott*